Hovering at a

Low Altitude

CHANA BLOCH

Poetry

Mrs. Dumpty

The Past Keeps Changing

The Secrets of the Tribe

Translation

Yehuda Amichai, *Open Closed Open* (with Chana Kronfeld)

Yehuda Amichai, *The Selected Poetry* (with Stephen Mitchell)

Dahlia Ravikovitch, *A Dress of Fire*

Dahlia Ravikovitch, *The Window: New and Selected Poems*
(with Ariel Bloch)

The Song of Songs (with Ariel Bloch)

Criticism

Spelling the Word: George Herbert and the Bible

CHANA KRONFELD

Criticism

On the Margins of Modernism: Decentering Literary Dynamics

Translation

Yehuda Amichai, *Open Closed Open* (with Chana Bloch)

Dvora Baron, *"The First Day" and Other Stories*
(cotranslated and coedited with Naomi Seidman)

Edited Volumes

Contraversions: Jews and Other Differences
(series coeditor, with Daniel Boyarin and Naomi Seidman)

David Fogel and the Emergence of Hebrew Modernism
(coedited with Michael Gluzman and Eric Zakim)

Amia Lieblich, *Conversations with Dvora*
(coedited with Naomi Seidman)

HOVERING AT A
LOW ALTITUDE

THE COLLECTED POETRY OF

Dahlia Ravikovitch

TRANSLATED FROM THE HEBREW BY

CHANA BLOCH

AND

CHANA KRONFELD

W. W. NORTON & COMPANY

New York   London

NATIONAL
ENDOWMENT
FOR THE ARTS
A great nation
deserves great art.

For information about permission to reproduce selections from this book,
write to Permissions, W. W. Norton & Company, Inc.,
500 Fifth Avenue, New York, NY 10110

For information about special discounts for bulk purchases, please contact
W. W. Norton Special Sales at specialsales@wwnorton.com or 800-233-4830

Manufacturing by Courier Westford
Book design by JAM Design
Production manager: Anna Oler

Library of Congress Cataloging-in-Publication Data

Ravikovitch, Dalia, 1936–2005.
[Poems. English.]
Hovering at a low altitude : the collected poetry of Dahlia Ravikovitch /
translated from the Hebrew by Chana Bloch and Chana Kronfeld.—1st ed.
p. cm.
ISBN 978-0-393-06524-4 (hardcover)
1. Ravikovitch, Dalia, 1936–2005—Translations into English.
I. Bloch, Chana, 1940– II. Kronfeld, Chana. III. Title.
PJ5054.R265A2 2009
892.4'16—dc22

2008054944

W. W. Norton & Company, Inc.
500 Fifth Avenue, New York, N.Y. 10110
www.wwnorton.com

W. W. Norton & Company Ltd.
Castle House, 75/76 Wells Street, London W1T 3QT

1 2 3 4 5 6 7 8 9 0

For Amichai Kronfeld ז"ל

(1947–2005)

in loving memory

Contents

Issues in Contemporary Judaism

MOTHER AND CHILD (1992)

Introduction

⟪෨⟫

WHEN DAHLIA RAVIKOVITCH died suddenly in August 2005 in Tel Aviv at the age of sixty-eight, her death was front-page news in Israel, and was met with an outpouring of grief from every corner of society. One of the great Hebrew poets of our time—indeed, many believe, the greatest Hebrew woman poet of all time—she was widely honored for her artistry and admired for her courage as a peace activist.

Ravikovitch's first book of poems, *The Love of an Orange*, published in 1959, created a literary sensation. While these poems expressed an utterly contemporary sensibility, it was their rare diction and archaic cadences, distilled from the most ancient layers of biblical Hebrew, that made readers marvel. That such stylistic mastery was the work of a twenty-three-year-old poet—and a woman at that—added to her mystique. *The Love of an Orange* immediately established Ravikovitch as one of the leading poetic voices of the post-1948 Statehood Generation, alongside her elders, Yehuda Amichai and Natan Zach. This was followed by five collections, *Hard Winter* (1964), *The Third Book* (1969), *Deep Calleth* (1976), *True Love* (1987), and *Mother and Child* (1992); the comprehensive collection *The Complete Poems So Far* (1995), whose publication was a major event in Israeli cultural life; and *Half an Hour before the Monsoon* (1998), the last book of poetry to appear in her lifetime. She also published three short story collections, *Death in the Family* (1976), *Winnie Mandela's Soccer Team* (1997), and *Come and Gone* (2005), eight books of children's verse and ten translations of children's classics by women authors, as well as translations of English poetry. A posthumous volume, *Many Waters: Poems 1995–2005*, edited by Dana Olmert and Uzi Shavit, appeared in 2006.

No other Hebrew poet, with the exception of the late Yehuda Amichai, has been so universally embraced by Israelis, whatever their ideological leanings. Ravikovitch's poems, like Amichai's, have been integrated into all facets of Israeli public life—set to music and adapted in theatrical productions, experimental films, dance performances, and art exhibits—and translated into twenty-three languages, including Arabic, Chinese, French, German, Hungarian, Russian, Serbo-Croatian, Vietnamese, and Yiddish. Enormously influential for several generations of Hebrew poets, and particularly empowering for younger women writers, her work has long been a staple of the Israeli school curriculum, required reading for matriculation exams, and the subject of scholarly research. But it has also reached many people who are not ordinarily readers of poetry. And despite its oppositional stance, her poetry has been appropriated by Israeli politicians past and present, who are given to reciting it on public occasions. She received all the major Israeli literary awards, culminating in 1998 in the Israel Prize, the highest national honor. The judges' citation noted: "[Ravikovitch] has been a central pillar of Hebrew lyric poetry during the fifty years of statehood. . . . Her poems are, on the one hand, a personal testimony of loss, impossible love and the desperate struggle for existence, and on the other, an expression of universal truth and the experiences of many. Her work is characterized by the synthesis of rich, elevated language with the colloquial idiom, and of a personal outcry with that of the collective. . . . This has made her the preeminent Hebrew poet of our time."

Dahlia was born in 1936 in Ramat Gan, a suburb of Tel Aviv. She inherited her love of poetry from her father, Levi, a Russian-born engineer, who emigrated to Palestine via China in the early 1930s. An abiding interest in the traditional Jewish texts—the very ones that women were barred from studying in earlier generations—was imparted to her by her mother, Michal, whose grandfather, Rabbi Shmuel Hominer, was among the founders of the Ultra-Orthodox neighborhood of Meah She'arim in Jerusalem in 1874. Though secular herself, Michal was a graduate of a religious teachers' college and taught Jewish studies. In 1942, when Dahlia was six, her father was run over by a drunken Greek soldier in the British army (see the poem "On the road at night there stands the man"). Shortly thereafter, Michal moved with her daughter and twin infant sons to Kibbutz Geva without telling the children of their father's death; Dahlia learned of it, traumatically, two years later on the kibbutz playground. Unable to adapt to the collectivist pressures of the kibbutz environment, she left on her own for Haifa at age thirteen, living with one foster family after another.

In Haifa Dahlia had the good fortune to be mentored by her high school literature teacher Baruch Kurzweil, who was soon to become an important figure in Israeli cultural life ("They're Freezing Up North"). Kurzweil's glowing review of *The Love of an Orange*, praising the originality and intensity of her lyrical voice and her seamless integration of the archaic and the contemporary, would secure her place in the canon. With the encouragement of Avraham Shlonsky, the leading poet of the pre-State Hebrew modernists, and Leah Goldberg, the major woman poet of the time ("The Bullfrogs"), Dahlia began publishing poetry when she was just eighteen, while serving for a brief period in the army Signal Corps. She studied English literature and Hebrew linguistics at the Hebrew University in Jerusalem ("Who Art Thou, O Great Mountain") and was awarded a fellowship for literary studies at Oxford. Married and divorced twice, she lived for thirteen years with Haim Kalir, with whom she had a son, Ido, born in 1978 when she was forty-two; Dahlia was devastated when she lost custody of him in 1989. Her connection with Ido remained the central bond in her life, and it occasioned the most tender poems in her oeuvre. For many years, Dahlia lived in the same modest apartment in Tel Aviv near the Mediterranean, working on and off as a journalist, television and theater critic, high school teacher, and writer of popular song lyrics, barely managing to eke out a living despite her literary prominence.

Dahlia's fragile health and reclusiveness did not deter her from becoming deeply involved in the cause of Palestinian human rights. She often joined demonstrations against forced evacuations, land confiscation, and the mistreatment of women and children in the West Bank. She frequently spoke out on television and in print, condemning the messianic nationalist settlers, and didn't hesitate to confront Israel's leaders directly. One of her targets was the abuse of language in the political realm. Such activism required no small measure of courage. "Like deep-sea divers," she wrote, "most poets lead a high-risk life because they are compelled to listen with such scrupulous attention to the very essence of words." Her status as a beloved, unofficial poet laureate allowed her protest to carry some weight with the Israeli public. It is commonly believed that she became politically engaged in the wake of Israel's 1982 invasion of Lebanon, but in fact her activism began in the 1960s and continued all her life. The writer Yitshak Laor observes: "Unlike others who over the years have zigzagged politically, Dahlia remained consistent. Evil was always defined for her through the eyes of a defenseless child."

But Dahlia's presence in the public eye was not limited to the political sphere. Israelis were fascinated by her comings and goings; her reclusiveness and striking beauty lent her a kind of celebrity status. The color of the coat and shoes she wore to some reception or other were considered worthy of notice in the gossip columns. In 1996, when she consented for the first time to be interviewed about her personal history, the popular news daily

Yediot Acharonot published a four-page spread with banner headlines proclaiming: "Our Greatest [Woman] Poet Breaks Years of Silence." And on the eve of the publication of a volume of her autobiographical short stories, *Come and Gone* (2005), the magazine section of the same newspaper ran a six-page, in-depth piece about her life and times, "The Burden of Loneliness." The public was well aware that Dahlia struggled all her life with clinical depression. Not surprisingly, perhaps, when she died suddenly in 2005, it was at first assumed that she had taken her own life. The pathologists' reports, however, definitively ruled out suicide and determined heart failure to be the cause of her death.

The loss and displacement of Dahlia's early years shaped her social sensibilities and informed all her writing. "If I didn't know depression myself, I wouldn't be able to feel the tears of the oppressed," she said in an interview. "On the road at night there stands the man" enacts the compulsion to visit and revisit the scene of childhood trauma:

> On the road at night there stands the man
> Who once upon a time was my father.
> And I must go down to the place where he stands
> Because I was his firstborn daughter.
>
> Night after night he stands alone in his place
> And I must go down and stand in that place.
> And I wanted to ask him: Till when must I go.
> And I knew as I asked: I must always go.

Although "On the road at night there stands the man" clearly sets forth a personal narrative, its meaning is not limited to the biographical. The poem is also a psychological exploration of the workings of trauma and a meditation on love and death, culminating in a reflection about the limits of language:

> And even though I was his firstborn daughter
> Not one word of love can he speak to me.

As with the work of other women poets, it has been tempting for critics to read every detail of Ravikovitch's biography into her poems. But even poems that deal with despair and death must not be reduced to a simplistic biographical reading; many of these have social and political implications that such a reading allows us to ignore (e.g., "Like Rachel," "Many Waters"). Dahlia herself tried to deflect attention from her personal history. "If you were to write an autobiography," she was asked in an interview, "how would you title it?" She answered: *What Must Be Forgotten. Whatever happened to me, aside from the poems, must be forgotten.*"

*   *   *

POWER AND POWERLESSNESS is Ravikovitch's defining subject: the devastating consequences of unequal power relations for the individual and for society, the self in a state of crisis refracting the state of the nation. While she is best known for her poems about the twists and turns of the human psyche and the passionate tension between eros and thanatos, she also explores questions of ethics, aesthetics, and social justice with analytical precision. All of this is accomplished with poetic nuance and a subtle hand, held in check by skepticism and a profound humility about her task as a poet. Her early work articulates the asymmetries of power in poems about fathers and daughters, men and women, kings and their subjects ("A Wicked Hand," "Clockwork Doll," "On Account of a King"). The later work focusses more intently on the precarious position of women ("Cinderella in the Kitchen") and, with increasing directness, the plight of Palestinians under the Occupation ("Lullaby").

A raw openness to pain, her own pain and that of others, hurts her into poetry, as Auden famously said of Yeats. In her favorite poem, "The Dress," the speaker is made to wear a dress that, like Medea's vengeful gift to Jason's wife, will consume her very flesh:

> What will become of you, she said,
> they made you a burning dress.
> They made me a burning dress, I said. I know.
> So why are you standing there, she said, you ought to beware.
> Don't you know what that means, a burning dress?
>
> I know, I said, but not to beware.

In "We Had an Understanding" there is no buffer at all between self and world—as if she had a "transparent skin, skin that doesn't protect the flesh, / not in the least." For her, however, this acute vulnerability cannot but engender an ethical imperative:

My protest is not in bitterness.
It is a cat's paw. At its tips are claws.

. . . .

Too long have we bemoaned the soul's suffering
with the muted meekness of the weak.
"Hamlet, Supreme Commander"

Ravikovitch is cherished for her love poems—a curious fact, since the
only poem where the lovers express their reciprocal passion features "two
fishes" ("Love"). Sometimes the relationship is merely a figment of the
speaker's imagination; in "Light and Darkness" the object of her fantasies
is a stranger waiting for another woman in an apartment across the way.
The yearning for a man who is all too often absent ("The Seasons of the
Year," "Trying," "Crane") echoes the yearning for the missing father ("The
Central Pillar," "Knowledge Comes Easy to the Wise"). When there is a
real man beside her in bed, he is described in distinctly unflattering terms
("He Crashed before Takeoff"). And even in the magical ecstatic "Delight,"
it is not the beloved but eros itself that is given presence and agency; desire
is cosmic, though the speaker's pleasure is personal and embodied:

And the wheel of the eye craved the sunwheel that day.
Then did I know a delight beyond all delight.

It is the light, not a male lover, that consumes her in this poem: "It would
swallow my head like a golden orange, that light." Love, indeed, is often
viewed as all-consuming, leaving the woman nothing of herself:

There a man loved me
Didn't leave me a fingernail.
"The Roar of the Waters"

But the recurrent motif of being devoured is reversed in love poems where
the woman speaker unabashedly declares her desire to engulf and incor-
porate the man, to make him part of herself. "The Second Trying" begins
with a wish: "If I could only get hold of the whole of you." Here and else-
where, the romantic template enables Ravikovitch to explore philosophi-
cally the relation of self to other:

If one could only get hold of the-whole-of-you-now,
How could you ever be for me what I myself am?

A lighter touch characterizes the poems filled with love for her son Ido (the section "No Stitchery More Precise" in *True Love*, "Child Boy Man," "Etc. Etc.," "More on the Matter of Ido"). From early on, in fact, poems of sprightly exuberance punctuate the various collections, displaying Ravikovitch's playful sense of humor ("A little woman made the world," "Tirzah and the Whole Wide World," "Magic Spells"). In "Portrait" the humor is rueful and self-directed:

> She sits in the house for days on end.
> She reads the paper.
> (Come on, don't you?)
> She doesn't do what she'd like to do,
> she's got inhibitions.
> She wants vanilla, lots of vanilla,
> give her vanilla.

Ravikovitch's emotional reach as a poet is wide, from savage sarcasm, pointed irony, and restrained pathos to prickly ambivalence, ebullient playfulness, and self-deprecating humor. Although her poems often deal with "extreme states of personal life: desolation, loss, estrangement, breakdown," in the words of the late Irving Howe, she is "a poet of wit, severe and costly," and her "language bristles with sharpness." Irony is among the many distancing devices (others include strict form, unreliable narrators, dialogue, archaism, and myth) that Ravikovitch employs to hold pathos in check. Even when she writes about despondency and death, she doesn't shy away from the astringent or irreverent. "It seems he specialized in death as a subject," she briskly sums up the life of a man who "couldn't pull himself out of despair" ("Do or Die"). And when addressing the recently deceased Yona Wallach, the major woman poet of the younger generation, she dares to express relief at the space her rival's death opens up for her own poetic voice. Yet this bluntness, as well as the speaker's sarcastic tone and gutsy refusal to join in the chorus of hypocritical praise, constitute a true homage to Wallach's convention-defying poetics:

> Yona, *shalom*,
> this time I'm the one who's talking
> and you won't interrupt anymore.
> Now, God help us, you're in the ranks of the holy and pure.
>
> . . . .
>
> you are one dead girl.

.　.　.　.　.　.　.　.

A good little girl from a proper home
knows to keep her mouth shut.
Doesn't utter a peep.

"Finally I'm Talking"

But her characteristic sharpness and irreverence do not preclude compassion, as the ending of the poem reveals. Nor do they preclude a serious intent. Witness the tongue-in-cheek title *Sugiyot be-yahadut bat-zmanenu*, "Issues in Contemporary Judaism," that she chose for the section of *True Love* (1987) devoted to political poems. The word for "issue," *sugiya*, can also refer to a Talmudic passage open to debate. To compare the rough-and-tumble of Israeli public life with the logic of rabbinical argument may seem at first glance to be merely satirical; at the same time, however, it has the effect of invoking Jewish law as an ethical criterion. "Marina Haddad" (2005), a poem about a Palestinian girl found dead and TV reporters who are concerned only with getting the right sound bite, is saved from preachiness by the speaker's wry commentary. Here the parodic use of academic jargon, while undercutting the pathos, reinforces the poem's clear-eyed analysis:

All the makings were there: bereavement, sorrow,
the mother a single parent,
the state of the nation as metonymy
for the fate of the individual (especially vice versa).

*　　*　　*

RAVIKOVITCH'S WORK, spanning half a century, exhibits an extraordinary stylistic range. The poems in her first two books (1959, 1964) employ traditional forms and an archaizing language resonant with biblical and liturgical echoes ("The Central Pillar") alongside experimental verse that invokes surrealist parable, avant-garde opera ("Outrage," "The Love of an Orange"), and folk genres such as ballads, fables, and nursery rhymes ("The Dove"). All of these combine in ways that may prove surprising to a reader of contemporary English poetry accustomed to speech rhythms and free verse. From 1969 on, with the publication of *The Third Book*, Ravikovitch renounces some of these rhetorical riches for a charged plain speech that draws primarily on modern Hebrew diction and colloquial idiom. Her work increasingly samples political slogans, military lingo, Israeli pop songs, even Yiddish lullabies, all the while maintaining its engagement with the traditional Jewish sources.

The densely allusive texture of Ravikovitch's poetry is enriched by references to ancient Near Eastern deities (El, Dagon, Baal-Zebub, Reshef, Yam) and Greco-Roman mythological figures (Medea, Prometheus). Her work, early and late, also engages in dialogue with English and American poetry, from Shakespeare, Blake, and Keats, through Dickinson, Hopkins, Yeats, Stevens, and Eliot, to Thomas, Sexton, and Plath. Her intimacy with the English canon is evident in her deft translations of the Scottish Ballads and of Poe, Yeats, and Eliot.

From the post-biblical Jewish tradition Ravikovitch adopts an array of voices and styles ranging from rabbinic legalism to Kabbalistic incantation, and from midrashic parable to liturgical poetry. For the American reader it may be difficult to understand why a poet for whom the question of faith doesn't even arise would draw so heavily upon the sacred Jewish texts. This is not an issue for an Israeli audience, since secular rewritings of the sacred have by now become the norm in modern Hebrew literary culture, in no small part thanks to poets like Amichai and Ravikovitch. But whereas Amichai constructs a systematic counter-theology, Ravikovitch doesn't even treat the Jewish God as a literary character. With the important exception of one poem, "The End of the Fall," God for her is reduced to appearances in quotations, expletives, and exclamations.

The canonical texts, above all the Bible, lend her poems their astonishing resonance. Sometimes simply a word—"dove," "potsherd," "whirlwind," "tarry"—can summon up an entire universe of discourse. In the early poetry, Ravikovitch shows a preference for the most ancient layers of biblical Hebrew, already marked within the Bible itself as archaic. Throughout her oeuvre, she is drawn to rare and arcane biblical expressions whose emotive import is strong even when their exact meaning remains mysterious. These ancient locutions paradoxically offer her a way of making her language new. A case in point is her penchant for *hapax legomena*, words or expressions that appear only once in the Bible. "The Love of an Orange," the title poem that opens Ravikovitch's first book, is a fable about the passion of an orange for the man who devours it:

> An orange did love
> The man who ate it,
> To its flayer it brought
> Flesh for the teeth.

The word we have translated "flesh" (Heb. *barot*, from the root *b.r.h.*, associated with eating) appears only once in the Bible in this form, in Lamentations 4:10. When *barot* is used in "The Love of an Orange," it immediately invokes one of the most horrific scenes in the Bible, where women are reduced to eating their own children during the siege of Jerusalem. That word alone is enough to summon up the grisly suggestion of cannibalism, amplifying the tension between eros and thanatos that is the poem's main theme.

The books of the Hebrew Bible that are in poetic form—the Psalms and Song of Songs, the Wisdom books (Proverbs, Ecclesiastes, and Job) and the Prophets—offer Ravikovitch a model for the lyric where public and private, political and philosophical dwell comfortably together. Psalm verses weave in and out of her poems; she often goes back to "Day unto day uttereth speech, and night unto night showeth knowledge" (Psalm 19:2) and to "Deep calleth unto deep at the noise of thy cataracts; all thy breakers and waves have surged over me" (Psalm 42:7). The Psalmist's yearning becomes a template for her own; in the poem "Day unto Day Uttereth Speech" King David himself, traditionally considered the author of the Psalter, joins her in song. The prophet Ezekiel's ecstatic visions of the divine offer her a metaphor for the workings of the poetic imagination:

> And I look, and behold:
> opening, revolving,
> entire worlds within the room.
> "The Beginning of Silence"

The genre of the *mashal*—a fable, parable, or exemplary tale ("Pride")— also serves her as a lyrical model, and she often assumes the voice of the sage in Wisdom literature:

> And I set my heart to learn:
> He who departs for an hour is as good as gone forever.
> "Heartbreak in the Park"

Her use of these traditional texts is never pious; in fact, it is typically ironic and irreverent. Her acerbic tone mocks the didactic analogies of the sages in "Two Garden Songs," where she turns a humorous but sympathetic eye on the busy little ants (not coincidentally feminine in Hebrew), whose mighty labors yield such measly results:

Some ants found half a carcass of a fly
and what a time they had
hauling it out of the grass.
Their little hips nearly split with the labor.

. . . .

I knew the ants would come to a bitter end—
all that hard work and an early death.

Here she pokes fun at the famous exhortation to the lazy in Proverbs 6:6–8: "Go to the ant, thou sluggard; consider her ways and be wise"; indeed, many of her biblical allusions are subject to witty reversals of this kind.

While Ravikovitch's biblical allusions can be ironic and even iconoclastic, there is nothing ironic about the way she invokes the ethical precepts of the prophets, whose critical voice and class sensibility resonate for her with the egalitarian ethos of the Israel of her childhood. She often chooses to foreground those prophetic texts that warn about the moral costs of social injustice. Informing her entire poetic outlook is Jeremiah's exhortation:

Thus says the Lord: Act with justice and righteousness, and deliver from the hand of the oppressor anyone who has been robbed. And do no wrong or violence to the alien, the orphan, and the widow, or shed innocent blood in this place (Jer. 22:3, NRSV).

In "A Jewish Portrait" she quotes verbatim Isaiah 1:12, a condemnation of the empty piety that masks unethical conduct:

She has no use for this business, Jerusalem.
Day after day they wrangle over the Temple Mount,
each man smites and reviles his brother,
and the dead prophet shrieks,
Who hath required this at your hand, to trample My courts?

One compelling reason for Ravikovitch's sustained dialogue with Jewish sources is her commitment to rescue them from the hands of religious zealots and sloganeering politicians, and to recover from within Judaism a secular ethical compass for her culture.

For a woman poet to speak in the wrathful and uncompromising voice of Jeremiah or Isaiah is no simple matter, given the gender politics of Jewish cultural history. Prophecy, one of the chief models for Hebrew poetry, is typically the domain of the male spokesman of God. The poet-as-prophet was a standard trope of earlier generations, associated especially with Chaim Nachman Bialik, the "national poet" of the Hebrew Revival period (1881–1920s), but male poets of later generations rebelled against this conception of their role. Women poets didn't have the luxury of such a rebellion, since the tradition did not afford them access to the poet-prophet voice. For Ravikovitch to claim the privileged stance of the prophet as her own, and what's more, to do so without accepting its authorizing divine source, amounted to a powerful feminist gesture.

Ravikovitch's poetry is often credited with launching Israeli feminism even before it became an explicit focus of social and cultural debate. Thus, for example, the editors of the important anthology *The Defiant Muse: Hebrew Feminist Poems from Antiquity to the Present* assert in their introduction that in Israel "poetry possibly preceded women activists in raising a feminist agenda. The greatest and most consistent contribution to the construction of a feminist consciousness in Israeli poetry is surely that of Dahlia Ravikovitch." As early as 1963, in an essay with the mock-traditional title "Women's Wisdom" (*Chokhmat nashim*), Ravikovitch uses the example of Emily Dickinson to challenge "the assumption that a woman's world is frail and restricted by nature."

"Clockwork Doll" (from the 1959 collection *The Love of an Orange*), the poem most frequently singled out as the paradigm example of Ravikovitch's feminism *avant la lettre,* is a closely rhymed sonnet in which the perfect outer form, like that of the mechanical doll, contrasts powerfully with an irreparable inner brokenness. The poem literalizes the stereotype of the "doll," which in both Hebrew and English slang of the 1950s refers to a pretty young woman, but grants her the sorry fate of Humpty Dumpty:

> I was a clockwork doll, but then
> That night I turned round and around
> And fell on my face, cracked on the ground,
> And they tried to piece me together again.
>
> Then once more I was a proper doll
> And all my manner was nice and polite.
> But I became damaged goods that night,
> A fractured twig poised for a fall.

Ten years later, in *The Third Book* (1969), Ravikovitch revisits this image in "The Marionette." The unreliable speaker of the first two stanzas, the helpless plaything of an invisible puppeteer, finds romance in her lack of freedom: "And the threads that wreathe my life / are genuine silk." Raviko-vitch then exposes the speaker's self-delusion, identifying the marionette with Mozart's Donna Elvira, seduced and betrayed by Don Giovanni but still pleading with him at the bitter finale. As in her other portraits of women, Ravikovitch does not simply reject the female stereotype but regis-ters its devastating psychological toll. She closes the poem with a sarcastic commentary on the condition of women in her own day:

> In the twentieth century, on a precious gray dawn,
> how fortunate to be a marionette.
> This woman is not responsible for her actions,
> the judges opine.
> Her fragile heart is gray as the dawn,
> her body hangs by a thread.

In her later poetry Ravikovitch moves increasingly toward understand-ing how women collude with their social marginalization in poems that often highlight the link between gender and class. In "Cinderella in the Kitchen" (1987) she calls into question the passive ideal of womanhood fostered by fairy tales, a genre that she herself found seductive in her early years. Her Cinderella finds an alternative to Prince Charming in the "infinite treasure" that filled her imagination. But whatever compensation it may afford, her "freedom of mind," such as it is, only reinforces her inertia:

> And she clenched her fists and said:
> I'm going off to war—
>
> Then dozed off in bed.

Sometimes the only power that the powerless have is in choosing how to die. In "Like Rachel" death is the ultimate form of refusal. Allusions to various figurations of Rachel reverberate throughout Ravikovitch's poetry, linking the matriarch of Genesis and Jeremiah's grieving Mother of the Nation with the modern Hebrew poet Rachel Bluvstein ("Rough Draft") to create a matrilineage of refusal and resistance. One Rachel whom Dahlia knew personally is Rachel Melamed-Eitan, the working-class mother of a fallen soldier who declares, echoing Jeremiah:

I am Rachel your mother
of clear mind and free will,
I will not be comforted.
                "But She Had a Son"

Ravikovitch resists the narrow nationalist construction of Rachel as a stand-in for the Jewish nation, portraying her instead as a flesh-and-blood mother. (Melamed-Eitan read this poem at Dahlia's memorial service, literally lending it her own voice.) In a move that is bolder yet, Ravikovitch puts Jeremiah's verse into the mouths of Palestinian mothers and grandmothers keening for their lost men. Modeling her poem on the Yiddish lullaby, she has them speak of themselves in the third person:

Mama and Grandma
a mournful old tune
will sing in Jabalya's cordon of gloom.

.   .   .   .

Rachel is weeping aloud for her sons.
A lamentation. A keening of pain.
                "Lullaby"

Critical consensus has it that until the early 1980s, with the exception of a poem or two, Ravikovitch's work centered on the personal. Her poetry, however, has always had a political dimension, though this is expressed very differently in the early and the late work. In the first four books, the political is often encoded in parables about far-off places (Australia, New Zealand, Chad, and Cameroon) and distant eras (King Solomon's reign, the Roman conquests, the Crusades). The Brechtian "How Hong Kong Was Destroyed" is set in an orientalized, surreal Hong Kong, where the rotting bodies of the prostitutes become analogous to the disintegrating modern metropolis. Manchuria serves as the setting for a decidedly antiheroic "A Private Opinion," written during the heady days following the 1967 war:

Heroes are something else again,

.   .   .   .

but let medals and badges not be their motive.
As a rule they're used for stoking up locomotives
as in Manchuria,
and I'm sorry to say they die like dogs.

"The Coming of the Messiah," which dramatizes the seductions and dangers of charismatic leadership, has been read as a critique of the messianic impulse of mainstream Zionism; according to the critic Hamutal Tsamir, it is set in the seventeenth-century Diaspora, when Jewish masses were captivated by the promises of the so-called false Messiah, Sabbetai Zevi. "Horns of Hittin," a cautionary tale about the then-new Israeli Occupation of Palestinian lands, goes back to the Crusades, always a fraught cultural symbol in the Middle East: "How cruel and naive those Crusaders were. / They plundered everything." When it was first published, this poem was immediately seen as provocative; the Israeli reader had no trouble decoding the referent of the poem's medieval "villagers" (*kafriyim*) as the official term for the rural Palestinian population. Dahlia herself told us that Yehoshafat Harkabi, a leading Israeli general and military historian, read this poem as a warning that the attempt to conquer another people could prove suicidal for the conqueror. Sometimes in these early works a phrase or two will suffice to link past and present, as in "The Hurling," where contemporary references to the muezzin and to Israeli border guards frame the description of Jerusalem in Solomon's times. In the haunting apocalyptic vision that closes the poem, all the king's power and all the king's wealth cannot forestall the prophesied doom:

> Jerusalem the City of David was hurled away
> Like a finger lopped from the body.

The late 1970s marked a major turning point in the ways Ravikovitch articulated the political. This was a period of great upheaval in Israeli society (referred to as *Ha-Mahapakh*, "The Overturning"), when Menachem Begin's right-wing Likud rose to power for the first time, routing the Labor Party. An unprecedented economic crisis ensued when, at the instigation of Milton Friedman, the government abruptly converted the economy to stock-market-driven capitalism. This was followed in short order by Israel's incursions into Lebanon, culminating in the 1982 invasion. The crisis in the national sphere contrasted sharply with the profound personal joy and fulfillment this period held for Dahlia: the birth in 1978 of her son Ido, the "true love" in the title of her 1987 book of poems. The confluence of these events made Ravikovitch's sensitivity to the oppression of the weak even more palpable, and from then on motherhood, feminism, and peace activism became inextricably linked for her.

At a writers' conference in Berkeley in 1989, we asked Dahlia what made her turn so forcefully to political concerns in her recent poetry.

"Until the 1982 Lebanon war," she said, "I managed somehow to go on living inside a bell jar. But then suddenly, all at once, when the invasion started, the bell jar shattered. Now there's no wall between personal and political. It all comes rushing in." She was frank about the reception of her political poems in Israel: "There has been a lot of protest, because those poems seem to some readers like an admission of guilt," she told us. "But as for me, I'm happy with them. I want to do something. I can't stand my impotence." In a 2004 television interview she elaborated: "Because I hold an Israeli passport, I have a share in all the wrongs that are done to the Palestinians. . . . I want to be able to say that I did all I could to prevent the bloodshed."

The last twenty-five years of her life mark the crowning achievement of Ravikovitch's poetic project—the period when the private and the public merge with extraordinary expressive force in her work. Now she is haunted by the inseparability of concerns with war, woman, and child. She explores the parallels between the plight of the Palestinians, the suffering of Jews in the Diaspora, and the constraints on women in patriarchal society, all the while resisting identity politics by deliberately blurring the boundaries between self and other ("A Jewish Portrait"). Her heightened focus on abuse is accompanied by a keen awareness of the moral responsibility of the writer. It is notoriously difficult to write political poetry without lapsing into harangue. Ravikovitch meets this challenge head-on by situating the protest in the crosscurrents of her own conflicted life, expressing her own sense of guilt and complicity—a strategy that enables the wary reader to hear her out.

Although these poems can be very direct, even blunt in their message and tone, they remain subtle and complex in their verbal artistry, and maintain the densely allusive style that is Ravikovitch's hallmark. Consider, for example, two poems where she iconoclastically inverts references to Psalms that are among the most familiar sites of cultural memory. "Two Isles Hath New Zealand" (1987) presents a mock-idyllic fantasy of escape from the "murderousness" (line 20) surrounding her to the "green pastures" of Psalm 23—in New Zealand, no less, where the grass covers all traces of the massacre of the native population. "The Captors Require a Song" (1992) invokes Psalm 137, for two millennia the central text on the impossibility of singing the Lord's song in a state of exile and oppression. In a startling reversal, Ravikovitch presents the Israelis as captors who violently extract a song from the displaced Palestinians:

> Quick, sing us a new song,
> a song we will yank from your throat with pliers.

Finally, one of the last poems published in Ravikovich's lifetime, collected posthumously in *Many Waters*, has the polyvalent title, *Mi-zimrat ha-aretz,* which we render as "The Fruit of the Land." In biblical Hebrew, which is insistently present in the poem, *zimra* can mean "produce," "bounty" and "power," "might," though in modern usage it means "singing." The effect of the poem depends on the shocking metaphor of Israel's military might as its bumper crop. The different meanings of the word *zimra* combine in a cacophony of voices, a chorus of boasts and clichés about the bounty of the land:

> and we've got crates of napalm and crates of explosives,
> unlimited quantities, cornucopias,
> a feast for the soul, like some finely seasoned delicacy.

This poem displays the unmitigated harshness that characterizes the political poems of *Many Waters*—poems that constitute nearly half the volume, their rage barely masking a painful disillusionment.

During the 1948 war, a twelve-year-old Dahlia wrote a poem in rhyming quatrains challenging the anthem of Beitar, the Revisionist right-wing youth movement. The poem starts with the idealistic prediction that "When the Hebrew national shall prevail, / It shall ne'er be cruel," and ends with the assertion that a socialist, antiwar ethos is the people's "eternal" goal: "Its way shall be to create, to toil; / Murder shall it revile." Punning on *le-natze'ach* ("to win, prevail") and *netzach* ("eternity"), and contrasting through rhyme *netzach* and *retzach* ("murder"), these wartime quatrains also show glimpses of the extraordinary verbal artist Dahlia was to become.

In 1987 one can still hear the child's idealism and hopefulness behind the adult's shattering admission in "Two Isles Hath New Zealand":

> No point hiding it any longer:
> We're an experiment that went awry,
> a plan that misfired,
> tied up with too much murderousness.

These lines have become almost a mantra for the Israeli peace camp.

In *Many Waters*, Ravikovitch takes this poetics of bluntness to a new

31

level in poems that are meant to be profoundly disturbing to their audience. In many of these poems she sardonically adopts the voice of angry supporters or even perpetrators of violence. In Dana Olmert's words, the crass diction she flaunts in this book points up the "cheapening of language and the inarticulateness of Israeli culture as symptoms of something more fundamental: an utter disrespect for the Other." By speaking through these voices, Ravikovitch lets us experience from within, as it were, the corrosive brutality of a militarized society.

In her late poems, through a mostly female cast of characters, Ravikovitch reenacts the drama of Israel and Palestine. In *Mother and Child* (1992), the related poems "But She Had a Son" and "What a Time She Had" are about a grieving Israeli mother who loses her son in a questionable military operation. These are followed by "A Mother Walks Around," written from the point of view of a pregnant Palestinian woman who loses her fetus as a result of a beating by Israeli soldiers. Here Ravikovitch's ordering of the volume suggests a parallel between Israeli and Palestinian mothers united by their common loss. In "Lullaby," set to the rhythms of the Yiddish cradle song, a Palestinian mother and grandmother lament the violent death of the family's father. This is immediately followed by "Free Associating" with its pastiche of Zionist pioneer songs. Here the voices of Israeli boosterism rail against the poet for her constant fault-finding, though they too are haunted despite themselves by the memory of a man who was beaten to death. In the spirit of Ravikovitch's telling juxtapositions, when we arranged the poems in the posthumous *Many Waters* we paired "Marina Haddad," about a dead Palestinian girl and her grieving mother, with "The Poetics of Applying 'Moderate Physical Pressure,' " the sadistic monologue of an Israeli woman soldier who pretends to have had a child by the prisoner she is torturing.

*   *   *

MORE THAN ANY other poem by Ravikovitch, the unforgettable "Hovering at a Low Altitude" has come to represent the return to an ideologically engaged poetry of protest in the Israeli literature of the late 1970s. Because this is an epoch-making poem, integrating many of her personal and political themes (gender, violence, outrage, flight), we have chosen it as the title poem of this collection. "Hovering" presents two female characters and a man who, though offstage almost till the end, fills the space of the poem with his ominous presence. At the center of the scene is an innocent young shepherdess, presumably Arab, who is about to become a victim of rape and murder, and—hovering surrealistically overhead—an Israeli woman, the poem's narrator, who watches from a safe distance, repeating "I am not here" and claiming "I haven't seen a thing." By voicing this disclaimer in the first person, Ravikovitch presents herself as guilty of the same denial, thereby enabling us to confront our own.

The title, "Hovering at a Low Altitude" (*Rechifa be-gova namukh*), uses army Hebrew in the style of military briefings or news bulletins. In the context of the early 1980s, the phrase would typically refer to low-flying helicopters in hovering formations, patrolling over Southern Lebanon. Here, however, it is the female speaker who is hovering, floating midair as in a Chagall painting. But the title is also a brilliant double take: in Hebrew slang, "to hover" (*le-rachef*) means to be politically and emotionally detached. *Richuf* is a Tel Aviv state of mind, an Israeli version of "cool" that allows people to dissociate from the political "situation" (*ha-matzav*):

> I've found a very simple method,
> not so much as a foot-breadth on land
> and not flying, either—
> hovering at a low altitude.

Politically explicit though it is, "Hovering" is far from being a one-sided *J'accuse*. For those familiar with Ravikovitch's work, it reads as an unflinching self-critique of her early poetry, where a young woman often flees from an oppressive reality to exotic regions of the globe and the far reaches of the poetic imagination. Moreover, the poet's account of her contemporaries' disengagement carries an urgent ethical condemnation of the culture of political escapism. As Robert Alter writes: "The image of low-altitude hovering over an atrocity is an . . . effective emblem of the situation of the ordinary Israeli, knowing but choosing not to see certain terrible acts perpetrated by other Israelis, or even in the name of the nation; more generally, it is a parable of the moral untenability of detached observation in any political realm."

*   *   *

"HOVERING" IS PART of a complex recurring symbol of fantasy travel in Ravikovitch's work. Its manifold expressions include not only the poetic imagination and the aspiring mind but also a psychological dissociation from reality and an escape from the Israeli here and now. Images of the

West—"The Blue West," as she calls it in a 1964 poem—associate the West with the exotic Other (perhaps surprisingly for the American reader), as well as with the realm of dreams and aspirations:

> I want to reach beyond that hill,
>
> . . . .
>
> I want to break out of the depths of the earth,
>
> . . . .
>
> I want to reach the ends of thought
> Whose very beginnings
> Slash like a knife.
> I want to ascend to the fringes of the sun
> And not fall prey to the fire.

But poems that travel to Africa and Asia ("In Chad and Cameroon," "War in Zanzibar," "How Hong Kong Was Destroyed") depict the Western colonial presence as a contagion infecting both colonized and colonizer. At times, the diction and cadences of the most archaic stratum of biblical poetry turn the speaker's journey into a kind of time travel. While in her early work Ravikovitch writes of fantasy voyages to faraway places that are associated with art and the imagination, these poems are also—as the political turn in her later poetry makes clear—about literal escapes from Israeli reality ("Tirza and the Whole Wide World," "Australia"). The speaker may be the passenger, pilot, or captain, or even a plane or a ship. In Ravikovitch's world, more often than not, these vessels capsize or crash. In the title poem of *Many Waters,* the speaker's own breakdown merges with the image of the sinking ship of state, evoking Columbus's *Santa Maria*:

> This ship
> is the *Dahlia Maria.*
> She will sink today,
> she is sinking today.

*   *   *

DAHLIA RAVIKOVITCH SOMETIMES presents a mordant view of the writerly life ("Making a Living," "The Hope of the Poet"), but poetry and the imagination remain for her an essential human need, indispensable for survival. Celan famously wrote, echoing Mandelstam, "A poem . . . can be a message in a bottle sent out in the—not always greatly hopeful—

belief that it will wash up on heartland, perhaps." "A Bottle on the Waters" (1992), a supplication whose lofty Hebrew echoes the Yom Kippur liturgy, invokes Mandelstam and Celan to express Ravikovitch's humility about her task as a poet. But the final line, astonishing in its simplicity and directness, affirms the power of poetry:

> Still, where there's a bottle tossed into the water,
> there's hope
> that the palm of a hand will grasp it, an eye will behold it,
> a human being one day will say of it in wonder:
> I found a bottle.

A Note on the Translation

ANY TRANSLATION FROM Hebrew presents an unusual challenge. To begin with, Hebrew is a language with its roots in antiquity that was revived as a vernacular only about a hundred years ago, and modern Hebrew is an echo chamber that preserves, even in everyday speech, the resonance of all its historical layers. The simplest words may be charged with ancient, often sacred, significance. Ordinary terms may have multiple meanings and a wide range of nuances and symbolic valences, drawing on three thousand years of literary and religious use. Even a straightforward term like *bayit,* "house," "home," can also mean a stanza in a poem, the Temple in Jerusalem, and the national homeland; in biblical and rabbinic culture, it can be a common metaphor for the female body. We translate a word like *bayit* variously, as indicated by the context—e.g., "Temple" in "History of the Individual," "Home" in "The Captors Require a Song"—and spell out other meanings and implications of the word in our footnotes.

Modern Hebrew has the dynamic nature of a new vernacular, eager to enrich its means of expression from every available source. Since the triliteral root system of Hebrew creates a kind of "component awareness," both the archaic layers of the language and new-minted expressions are generally transparent to readers. Ravikovitch artfully exploits the tensions between the archaic and modern senses of a term. The verb *le-hitnachel,* for example, is usually understood in biblical Hebrew as "to inherit" or "settle down in" [the land]; in the contemporary Israeli context, however, the primary meaning is "to join a settlement in the Occupied Territories." In "Rough Draft," this word is a juncture between the personal and political meanings of the poem. When we asked Dahlia which of the two was primary for her, she told us: "Either way you lose something." Our solution here, as in a few other instances, is to use both: "not settle down, not be a settler."

Ravikovitch's diction ranges from the high formal to the crass demotic. In the early work, her contemporary idiom is saturated with archaic expressions as well as biblical, liturgical, and mythical references; indeed, many of the early poems have never before been translated for precisely this reason. In working with these tightly wrought poems, our challenge was to render her densely allusive style in English while retaining her freshness of expression and ironic modernist tone. In some of the late work Ravikovitch avails herself of a coarse slangy Hebrew—for example in "*Adloyada* in Manhattan," written in the voice of Israeli expatriates who "didn't remember so good how to speak Hebrew." It is the bits of realia in this poem, like the Adloyada of the title, that elude translation; we could only begin to adumbrate their cultural significance in our notes. The style itself, however, is less difficult to convey in English because crudity translates easily. Often we find the mix of formal and demotic in the very same poem. This would not be problematic for a reader of Hebrew, since Hebrew mixes stylistic registers and historical layers more easily than English.

In our translations we have tried to enlarge, if only slightly, the receptivity of English to otherness of style. We have endeavored to preserve Ravikovitch's syntax, which is marked by the frequent use of parallel clauses, anaphora, and the conjunction "and." Her sentence structures often echo the paratactic syntax of the Bible, proceeding by implicit analogy rather than grammatical subordination. In our translations we draw frequently upon the King James Version (KJV) for its diction, inversions, and archaic forms. Its historical importance for later poetry, indeed for modern English in general, gave us the wherewithal to add texture and avoid flatness of expression. We were delighted to be able to use Robert Alter's precise and elegant translations in *The Five Books of Moses, The David Story,* and *The Book of Psalms.* In rendering the poems' biblical allusions, we have on many occasions created an amalgam of several standard Bible translations, or provided our own literal versions, in order to convey more closely the meaning and nuance of the Hebrew. In our notes, our source was the KJV, unless otherwise specified. Occasionally we refer to the New Revised Standard Version (NRSV), the Revised English Bible (REB), or the Soncino Bible when those translations better reflect the Hebrew.

In order to avoid the tendency of English translations toward the bland and univocal, we chose to heighten the literary resonance of Ravikovitch's poems in English by turning to those poets who are particularly relevant for her, above all Shakespeare; she herself actually quotes verbatim four lines from Hamlet's "To be, or not to be" soliloquy in her poem "Hamlet, Supreme Commander." In "On Account of a King," for example, a parable set in the times of the Roman conquests, the soldiers are described in the Hebrew as having no time "to pamper their bodies under eiderdown"; we translated this as "to dally where the beds are soft," echoing *Antony and Cleopatra*. On several occasions we drew on other poets whose works form part of Ravikovitch's "poetic bookcase," from Sappho's "loosener of limbs" (see "Mahlon and Chilion") to Yeats's "gyres" ("Murmurings") and Lewis Carroll's "snark" ("Tirzah and the Whole Wide World"). Poems about the relation between reality and the poetic imagination in fact often engage the English and American canon directly; for example, "Even for a Thousand Years" starts with a reference to Stevens's "The Man with the Blue Guitar" and goes on to dispute Keats's "Beauty is truth, truth beauty." We have tried to indicate that engagement in our translations. At the same time, we were careful not to import facile parallels from American culture just to ease the task of the reader. We did attempt to assist the reader in ways we consider appropriate: highlighting gradations of tone; calling attention to irony, wit, and humor, which are often lost in translation; and working against the tendency to sentimentalize and exoticize Ravikovitch's voice.

One of our major challenges was the different status of meter and rhyme in English and Hebrew poetry. While modernism in English involved the repudiation of strict forms, this was not the case in Hebrew and many other literatures. Morever, Hebrew rhymes more easily than English since grammatical rhyme automatically results from suffixes marking gender, number, or person. This kind of easy rhyme, traditionally considered "bad" in Hebrew, was reclaimed by the poets of Ravikovitch's generation precisely because it was "unpoetic" and thus suited to ironic deflation and the restraint of pathos. Rather than impose an American aesthetic, our practice has been to retain the use of rhyme and meter wherever possible. Much of Ravikovitch's early poetry is written in a combination of full rhyme and grammatical rhyme and uses variations on metrically strict forms. We have introduced capital letters at the beginning of lines for her first two books to signal their more formal style (Hebrew has no capital letters). Where Ravikovitch employs rhyme in a sustained way, or locally for special effect, we strive for full rhyme, often adopting a modernist rhyme common in Hebrew, where two rhyming words share at least one full syllable but have a different final consonant. Where she uses grammatical or monorhyme, we opt for off-rhyme or repetition.

Hebrew is a language that genders everything, yet treats only the masculine as the norm. For a woman writer in particular, every grammatical choice becomes charged, a personification waiting to happen. Where the metaphorical narrative engendered by the grammar is vital to the meaning of the poem, we use the pronouns "he" or "she" though the English reader might expect "it" (e.g., "Blue Lizard in the Sun," "Lying upon the

Waters"). Where we cannot indicate gender through pronouns, we do so in our choice of diction. For example, in "Two Garden Songs" a little drama emerges between the idle loutish insects (Heb. *charakim,* masc.) and the hardworking ants (Heb. *nemalim,* fem.). Because the plural pronoun doesn't indicate gender in English, we call attention to the gendered aspects of the scene through our choice of adjectives and verbs: "A few *husky* insects *strutted* about in the grass, / *whistling* at those foolish ants."

*   *   *

THIS COLLECTION REPRESENTS the trajectory of Ravikovitch's life in poetry, the full range of her themes and styles from the 1950s, when she began writing, until her death in 2005. We have translated most of *The Complete Poems So Far* (1995), and nearly all of the posthumous collection *Many Waters: Poems 1995–2005*, edited by Dana Olmert and Uzi Shavit, omitting only a handful of poems that we found impossible to render as poetry in English. We follow Ravikovitch's arrangement of the poems in the former; in the latter, however, we have modified somewhat the order chosen by Olmert and Shavit. About a third of the poems appeared in earlier versions in *The Window: New and Selected Poems* (1989), which Chana Bloch translated in collaboration with Ariel Bloch. Every one of those translations has been extensively revised to convey more precisely nuances of meaning, allusion, and sound. Many of the poems in our collection have never before been translated into English; this is especially true of the formally challenging early poetry. Conversations with Dahlia in Tel Aviv, Jerusalem, and Berkeley, as well as her letters and written comments on earlier versions, have influenced our choices.

This book is in effect an annotated edition. In our extensive footnotes we elucidate linguistic ambiguities, references to texts, especially traditional Jewish texts that may not otherwise be transparent to the reader of English, and to Israeli realia. Our notes also refer the reader to internal allusions and significant recurrent images in Ravikovitch's oeuvre. Particularly when we are dealing with some matter of Jewish or Israeli culture, we are well aware that many of our notes point to a problem rather than resolving it; often a note will merely signal to the reader: "The following bit of culture-stuff, which we now define in a few words, is something that cannot be defined in a few words."

Given the imperial status of American English today, translations of poetry into English, especially from minor languages, run the risk of domesticating the foreign, blurring subversive features, or bleaching out any sign of cultural particularity. This is a tendency we have consciously tried to resist. We have benefited in this regard from recent developments in translation studies that move beyond metaphors of fidelity and betrayal to a model of intercultural negotiation, one that is keenly aware of asymmetries of power between languages.

Intercultural negotiation comes easily to us, given our backgrounds: Chana Bloch is an American poet and a translator of contemporary and biblical Hebrew; Chana Kronfeld is an Israeli-born scholar of Hebrew and comparative literature and translation studies, and a translator of contemporary Hebrew literature. As we worked together, we debated vigorously every possible meaning of the Hebrew text and every choice of diction or rhythm. Entirely shared is our pleasure in presenting to a wider audience a poet celebrated and much beloved in Israel who deserves to be more widely known.

Acknowledgments

⊗

THIS BOOK IS dedicated to the memory of Amichai Kronfeld ל״ז, who contributed to the project from its inception until just days before his untimely death. Amichai brought his keen mind and musician's ear to numerous drafts of the poems, writing detailed and penetrating notes that we continued to refer to even in our final revisions. His critiques were informed by his sensitivity to the nuances of the Hebrew language, its rhythms and meters, and above all, his lifelong love for Dahlia's poetry. In Dahlia's last letter to us—as it turned out, shortly before her own death—she warmly joined in this dedication.

Dahlia read the manuscript-in-progress and offered her enthusiastic approval of our work. We have greatly benefited over the years from conversations with her, as well as from her letters and written comments on early versions of the poems; we quote from some of these exchanges in our introduction and notes. It has been our pleasure to work closely with Ido Kalir, Dahlia's son, and Dana Olmert, coeditor of *Many Waters* and executor of Ravikovitch's literary estate; we deeply appreciate their cogent responses to all our questions and their graciousness in providing access to unpublished archival materials.

We are very fortunate to count among our closest friends a number of gifted poets, translators, and scholars who helped us with unstinting generosity. Anita Barrows read many versions of the translations as they emerged from our workshop and helped us nudge them into shape. Three friends undertook to read the entire manuscript; their comments have left an imprint on every page. Rutie Adler compared our versions closely with the Hebrew original, offering her linguist's perspective and her insights into the use of Jewish textual sources. Tess Gallagher's challenging questions and suggestions were informed by her imaginative reach as a poet and translator, and her uncanny ability to intuit the Hebrew. Gail Holst-Warhaft brought to her close reading of the manuscript her expertise as a musicologist and a translator of Greek poetry, ancient and modern, and

43

her exquisite sensitivity to inflections of rhythm, form, and archaic diction. Marcia Freedman applied her fine editorial skills to our introduction. Ani Mac gave us helpful feedback on the introduction. Daniel Boyarin, Yael Chaver, Terry Greenblatt, and Ron Hendel provided illuminating answers to textual queries. The indefatigable Eliyah Arnon came to the rescue early and often in matters ranging from temperamental computers to inscrutable references; his bibliographic research helped us flesh out our notes.

The Bible translations and commentaries of our friend and colleague Robert Alter were an invaluable resource; his consistent support has meant a lot to us. We have learned a great deal from recent research on Ravikovitch by Michael Gluzman, Hanan Hever, Barbara Mann, Allison Schachter, Chaya Shacham, Hamutal Tsamir, Meir Wieseltier, and Ofra Yeglin, as well as from Galit Hasan-Rokem, Tamar Hess, and Shirley Kaufman, the editors of *The Defiant Muse*. We occasionally borrowed an apt word from translations of individual poems published by Rachel Tzvia Back, Tsipi Keller, Gabriel Levin, and Rami Saari.

A Translation Fellowship from the National Endowment for the Arts provided financial support and much appreciated validation. Chana Kronfeld wishes to thank the University of California at Berkeley for a sabbatical leave that afforded her the gift of time. The graduate students in her seminar on Ravikovitch—Nitzan Keynan, Noam Manor, Riki Ophir, Shaul Setter, Zehavit Stern, Zohar Weiman-Kellman, and post-doctoral fellow Dahlia Gavrieli—offered perceptive critiques of translations-in-progress. Chana Bloch wishes to thank the Rockefeller Foundation's Bellagio Study Center and the Djerassi Resident Artists Program for providing ideal working conditions. The members of her poetry group—Sandra Gilbert, Jeanne Foster, Diana O'Hehir, Peter Dale Scott, Phyllis Stowell, and Alan Williamson—helped us improve some knotty passages.

The University of California at Berkeley hosted a memorial for Ravikovitch, which Judaica Librarian Paul Hamburg helped organize. On that occasion, many of our translations were presented publicly for the first time, a number in musical settings by Israeli composer Ron Weidberg and American composer John Schott. The students and faculty who participated in study sessions in preparation for this event gave us valuable feedback. Mills College and the Berkeley/Richmond Jewish Community Center hosted fruitful workshops on issues of translating Ravikovitch.

Our gratitude to Georges Borchardt, a prince among literary agents, who steered this project with his inimitable skill and good judgment. Early on, Grace Paley and Adrienne Rich recognized the importance of Ravikovitch's work; their encouragement meant a great deal to us.

It has been a true pleasure to work with W. W. Norton. We especially wish to thank our editor, Jill Bialosky, and her editorial assistant, Adrienne Davich, for their care and graciousness in bringing this project to fruition, and David Stanford Burr, our expert copyeditor.

Our thanks to the editors of the following journals and volumes, where earlier versions of the translations and a short section of the introduction first appeared: *Evansville Review* (cowinner of the Barnstone Translation Prize), *Feminist Studies, Jewish Quarterly, Judaism, Lyric Poetry Review, Nashim, The New Yorker, Nightsun, Poetry, Poetry International, The Progressive, Siecle 21* (in French translation), *Tikkun,* and *Two Lines.* Thanks as well to Peter Cole, editor of *Hebrew Writers on Writing,* Rachel Tsvia Back, editor of *With an Iron Pen,* and conceptual artist Jenny Holzer, who brought Ravikovitch's poetry to Rome's public spaces. Finally, thanks to Alan Mintz, editor of *Reading Hebrew Literature,* for permission to cite sections from Chana Kronfeld's article on "Hovering at a Low Altitude."

With unfailing good humor, our families allowed themselves to be pressed into service at a moment's notice. Chana Bloch's husband, Dave Sutter, offered incisive criticism of the introduction; he brought to the translations his discernment, wit, and love of poetry. Her sons, Benjamin and Jonathan, applied their gifts for poetry and language to problem solving with their usual alacrity of mind. Chana Kronfeld's daughter, Maya, was a source of life-giving joy. Her analytical rigor and linguistic insight were important resources as we worked on the introduction and the note on the translation, as well as on early versions of the poems. Amichai Kronfeld's aunt, Tikva Honig-Parnass, was an invaluable source of expertise on subtleties of sociological and cultural detail in Dahlia's poetry.

Finally, we wish to thank each other for the ongoing pleasures of "The Two Chanas" collaborative duo. We are grateful for an exhilarating conversation about poetry, language, and culture in which we keep learning from one another, and for a deepening friendship that enriches both our lives.

THE
LOVE
OF
AN
ORANGE

for my mother

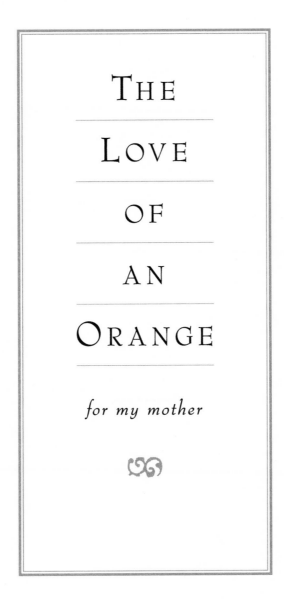

The Love of an Orange

An orange did love
The man who ate it.
A feast for the eyes
Is a fine repast;
Its heart held fast   5
His greedy gaze.

A citron did scold:
I am wiser than thou.
A cedar condoled:
Indeed thou shalt die!   10
And who can revive
A withered bough?

The citron did urge:
O fool, be wise.
The cedar did rage: 15
Slander and sin!
Repent of thy ways
For a fool I despise.

An orange did love
With life and limb   20
The man who ate it,
The man who flayed it.

※   ※   ※

Title, cf. Prokofiev's surrealist comic opera, *The Love for Three Oranges*, where oranges are objects of desire.

Lines 3–4, *feast for the eyes . . . repast*. Alludes to the Garden of Eden story, Gen. 2:9, 3:6. The Hebrew term for orange, *tapu'ach zahav*, literally translates as "golden apple."

Lines 7–18, *A citron . . . A cedar*. Modelled on Jotham's parable of the trees, Judges 9:8–15: "The trees went forth . . . and they said unto the olive tree"; cf. 2 Kings 14:9, "The thistle . . . sent to the cedar." Also echoing the recriminations of Job's "comforters."

An orange did love
The man who ate it,
To its flayer it brought 25
Flesh for the teeth.

An orange, consumed
By the man who ate it,
Invaded his skin
To the flesh beneath. 30

Line 26, *Flesh* (Heb. *barot*, lit. "food"). Lam. 4:10, a description of women eating their own children during the siege of Jerusalem. An example of *hapax legomenon,* i.e., a word that occurs in this form only once in the Hebrew Bible; on Ravikovitch's use of hapax, see introduction, pp. 23–24.

The Central Pillar

The Central Pillar

Among the four winds stands the central pillar,
The central pillar for all living souls,
Every soul bound in the bond of life
And the bond of life in the central pillar.

Every soul shall praise the Lord,   5
Shall have no end in the central pillar,
The central pillar of the rising sun,
The central pillar of the setting sun.

And every soul shall have no end.
Father's soul too in the central pillar,   10
And Father's soul like a flower that opens
From rising sun unto setting sun.

＊   ＊   ＊

Title, *The Central Pillar* (Heb. *amud ha-tikhon*). The repository of all souls, support-
ing the four points of the compass, lit. "the four winds of the heavens"; a Kabbalistic
concept. The poem is a mosaic of lines from the Psalms and liturgy, in particular the
Hallel prayer.

Lines 2–3, 5, *all living souls . . . bond of life . . . praise the Lord*. Conflating the Yiz-
kor (In Memoriam) liturgy, the morning prayer for Sabbath and holidays, and Psalm
150:6, the closing verse of the Psalter.

Lines 3, 5, 9, 13, 17, *Every soul* (Heb. *kol ha-neshama*). A sustained ambiguity, refer-
ring both to the souls of the dead and to living beings, i.e., those having the breath
(root *n-sh-m*) of life.

Lines 7–8, *rising sun . . . setting sun*. Psalm 113:3.

Every soul shall praise the Lord.
Praise ye the Lord in his faithful flock,
Praise ye the Lord in the bond of life,   *15*
Praise ye the Lord in the central pillar.

Every soul shall praise the Lord.
Indeed the dead praise not the Lord.
Father's soul in the central pillar
And its voice goes out to the end of the world.   *20*

Knowledge Comes Easy to the Wise

From Damascus town he'll come,
From the rivers Amanah and Pharpar;
Deceit is despised in his eyes,
He would not make a fool of me.

From the land of Cuthah he'll come,   *5*
In Kittim land be revealed;
He'll command a ship not his own
But he wouldn't make a fool of me.

He'll consort with sailors in the port,
He'll cast his charms upon them,   *10*
Win them with fawning words,
And their ship he will commandeer.

⁙   ⁙   ⁙

Line 14, *faithful flock* (Heb. *kehal chasidav*). Psalm 149:1.

Line 18, *the dead . . . the Lord.* Psalm 115:17.

Title, *Knowledge Comes Easy to the Wise.* Proverbs 14:6. The yearning for the missing father, drawing on biblical Wisdom literature, here an ultimately ineffectual source of reassurance.

Line 2, *Amanah and Pharpar.* 2 Kings 5:12. Lines 5–6, *Cuthah,* 2 Kings 17:24, *Kittim land,* Jer. 2:10, Ezek. 27:6. All sites in Ravikovitch's exotic geography of the imagination.

Their cunning will he exceed,
Their wisdom he'll carry off.
Surely, he vows, one day   *15*
He'll weigh gold into their palm.

Restive, he'll sail away
From that kingdom by the sea.
Confounded be the wit of fools
Who say: We took him for dead.   *20*

Knowledge comes hard to the fool.
They saw me as one deluded.
They said: Your father is deluding you.
No, he wouldn't make a fool of me.

Among galley men be it known,   *25*
Be it known and fathomed well,
Among Kittites who sail in fleets:
He would not make a fool of me.

Six Hundred Thirteen Commandments Plus One

> *Six hundred thirteen commandments were given to Israel*
> *and seven to the Sons of Noah.*
> *Even the dead are bound by one.*

And the dead man came home again
To tell his sons about his death
Lest they shudder to hear another tell
That horrifying tale.

*   *   *

Title, *Six Hundred Thirteen Commandments*. The number of dos and don'ts (Heb. *mitzvot*) specified in the Torah.

Never was there among the dead   5
Any who did as much.
Go forth and behold the graves of the dead:
Has anyone done as much?

He sat with us, he didn't stir,
All seven mourning days.   10
For how could he alone find peace
And leave us to our grief?

And so he told the tale of his death,
Expounding word by word,
For he believed that if we heard   15
We too might be consoled.

Albeit peace befits him now,
He will return if we entreat,
Never will he pass us by
Nor close his eyes to our pain;   20
He will shoulder an equal share
Of that horrifying tale.

Seven days and years without end,
Whene'er we demand it of him,
When we are overcome by grief,   25
He cannot help but come.

A Wicked Hand

Smoke rose in the slanted light
And my daddy was hitting me.
Everyone there laughed at the sight,
I'm telling the truth, and nothing but.

*   *   *

Line 26, *He cannot help but come.* Cf. Exod. 23:5, which enjoins one to help even an
enemy; see "Beheaded Heifer." The verb *azov*, which usually means "to leave," is used
in this biblical verse in the sense of "to help."

Smoke rose in the slanted light.   5
Daddy slapped the palm of my hand.
He said, It's the palm of a wicked hand.
I'm telling the truth, and nothing but.

Smoke rose in the slanted light
And Daddy stopped hitting me.   10
Fingers sprouted from the wicked hand,
Its works endure and will never end.

Smoke rose in the slanted light.
Fear singes the wicked hand.
Daddy stopped hitting me   15
But that fear endures and will never end.

"On the road at night there stands the man"

On the road at night there stands the man
Who once upon a time was my father.
And I must go down to the place where he stands
Because I was his firstborn daughter.

Night after night he stands alone in his place   5
And I must go down and stand in that place.
And I wanted to ask him: Till when must I go.
And I knew as I asked: I must always go.

In the place where he stands, there is a trace of danger
Like the day he walked that road and a car ran him over.   10
And that's how I knew him and marked him to remember:
This very man used to be my father.

       *   *   *

Line 11, *marked him to remember* (Heb. *natati bo simanim*). Evoking a phrase from
the Passover Haggadah where Rabbi Judah is said to have "made a mnemonic device"
to recall the ten plagues.

Not one word of love does he speak to me
Though once upon a time he was my father
And even though I was his firstborn daughter
Not one word of love can he speak to me.

The Land of the Setting Sun

꧁꧂

The Land of the Setting Sun

> *He removed the horses that the kings of Judah had*
> *dedicated to the sun, at the entrance to the house of the*
> *Lord, . . . then he burned the chariots of the sun with fire.*
> —2 Kings 23:11

There's a road to the land of the setting sun, so I was told.
But whether I might enter that land
I was never told.

No one would come with me on that road, so I set out alone
To find the land where the setting sun   5
Rides his chariot of gold.

Magnificent kings, kings without peer, so I was told,
Ruled the land of the setting sun
In the days of old.

And I said in my heart: If I come to the land of the setting sun   10
I shall be given a robe of purple,
A throne of gold.

*   *   *

Title, *The Land of the Setting Sun*. Cf. Zech. 8:7, usually translated "the west country."
Cf. also Psalm 113:3, "The Central Pillar," and "The Blue West."

Epigraph, 2 Kings 23:11 (NRSV). Recounting King Josiah's purge of pagan artifacts
from Temple worship. Cf. Exod. 20:4, also read as a general prohibition on visual art.

In the land of the setting sun, I shall find lasting peace.
—That's a tale I spun alone.
That tale I was never told.   *15*

Savior

There once was a man sick unto death
And his sickness waxed exceeding sore.
And he waited long for his savior to come
For he said in his heart: My savior will come.

And his brother did say: His savior will come.   *5*
And his uncle did say: His savior will come.
As to their kinsman, they paid him no heed
For they said in their hearts: His savior will come.

And so that man kept wasting away,
Wasting away from day to day.   *10*
Still he spake no ill of his brother
For he said in his heart: My savior will come.

And he lay on the bed whereon he would die
With trust in his heart: My savior will come.
All day he spake only: Savior, savior.   *15*
Who is not able to pronounce that word?

And his brother said: Indeed he will come,
This day or the next his savior will come,
I trust in my heart his savior will come.
Outside a man howled: "No savior, none!"   *20*

*   *   *

Line 16, *not able to pronounce that word* (Heb. *lo yakhin le-daber ken*). Citing verbatim
Judges 12:6, where during a civil war the tribesmen who were not able to pronounce
shibboleth correctly were thrown to their death.

58

And the sick man kept wasting away
Yet all his refrain was: Savior, savior.
Still he would not speak ill of his brother
For he was not able to pronounce those words.

The Coming of the Messiah

I

People stood at their doorstep all night long,
Waiting for their Messiah all night long.
They'd sold their houses to strangers with full assent:
Messiah is not like everyman that he should repent.

The Faithful:
If you do not come to us,   5
Who shall come?
Can we have trusted: Come thou!
And he not come?
If we've sold the household goods we owned
And all our possessions have we pawned   10
And all our silver bound, in hand,
As those who uproot themselves from this land—
And here we stand at the door of our home
That nevermore shall be our home
To await the coming of the guest divine,   15
Shall he not come?

If you do not come to us,
Who shall come?
Can we have entreated: Come thou!
And he not come?   20

Line 3, *They'd sold their houses.* As did masses of European Jews, enthralled by the so-called false Messiah, Sabbetai Zevi (1626–1676). This poem has been read as an early critique of the messianic impulse of mainstream Zionism (see introduction, p. 29).

Line 4, *Messiah . . . repent.* Num. 23:19, "God is not a man . . . that he should repent."

II

At their doorstep they waited all that night
But Messiah came not to guide them aright.
Is Messiah indeed like everyman who has erred?
For did he not rue and repent of his word?

The Faithful:
Doth a dead men's field   25
Entrap the living?
Doth a dead men's field
Swallow up the living?
Lo, our houses now are sold,
And unto others falls our gold,   30
And our land like a field of the dead, 'tis true.
They are the many, and we the few.

Doth a dead men's field
Entrap the living?
Doth a dead men's field   35
Swallow up the living?

Royal Gifts

The King went down with his beloved
Down to the ship's deep hold
Down to the ship's deep hold
To choose her a gift from his treasures of gold.

*   *   *

Line 28, *Swallow up*. A reference to the story of Korah, Num. 16:30–33, "And the earth opened its mouth, and swallowed them up."

Title, *Royal Gifts*. The Queen of Sheba's visit to King Solomon: "And when the queen of Sheba heard of the fame of Solomon . . . , she came to prove him with hard questions. [She brought him gifts of] very much gold, and precious stones. . . . And King Solomon gave unto the queen of Sheba all her desire, . . . beside that which Solomon gave her of his royal bounty" (1 Kings 10:1–13; cf. 2 Chron. 9:1–12). According to popular lore, their encounter was both intellectual and erotic.

—Sheba, I'll give thee horsemen and footmen,   5
A palace of prayer unto thee I plight,
Thy prayer unto God shall I recite,
E'en thy prayer—for love of thee.

Ivory and parrots shall I grant thee.
Elders and sages shall attend thee.   10
Whatever in wisdom I searched and weighed
I'll reveal unto thee—for love of thee.

Dwarfs and Cushites I shall grant thee,
Chariots of Sheba, its prince and squire.
Thy head shall wheel from my keen desire.   15
E'en the head stone shall I grant thee.

Chorus:
The head stone, the head stone,
Happy is he who makes it his own.

—O King, that stone is already my own,
The chariots of Sheba, its prince and squire.   20
My head doth wheel and whirl with desire
To stroke the head stone
To lick the head stone
To crush the head stone.

All my desire I took for my own   25
And by degrees my desire hath grown
Insatiable, my desire grew bold
Partaking six and sevenfold.
I want the head stone
To stroke the head stone   30

Line 13, *Cushites*. From the land of Cush. Traditionally both Cush and the land of
Sheba have been identified as Ethiopia.

Line 16, *head stone*. A building's keystone, as in Zech. 4:7, where it is an architectural
image referring to the Temple. Also symbolic of the phallus and the Logos.

Line 25, *All my desire*. Psalm 38:9, "Lord, all my desire [lit. 'lust'] is before thee."
Ravikovitch returns the term to its erotic sense here.

To lick the head stone
Butt my head on the head stone.

My desire shall yet be my ruin.
Behold, the day of my death is upon me.
All my desire shall I pour before thee—   35
I want the head stone
To stroke the head stone
To crush the head stone.
All this is upon my head now,
My very own head   40
        And neck now.
I knew my desire would be my ruin.

The King is the head stone.
From the ship's deep hold to the ends of the world,
How vile a thing, his attendants are blind.   45
Can they not see the fire
Going forth from the bramble,
Burning in their King?

The King is the head stone.

Chorus:
The head's stone, the head stone,   50
Woe unto him who takes it for his own.

Line 47, *bramble*. From the parable of Jotham, Judges 9:14–15.

Clockwork Doll

Clockwork Doll

I was a clockwork doll, but then
That night I turned round and around
And fell on my face, cracked on the ground,
And they tried to piece me together again.

Then once more I was a proper doll   5
And all my manner was nice and polite.
But I became damaged goods that night,
A fractured twig poised for a fall.

And then I went out to dance at the ball
But they cast me aside with the dogs and the cats   10
Though all my steps were measured and true.

And my hair was golden, my eyes were blue
And I had a dress with flowers and all,
And a sprig of cherries tacked to my hat.

Line 8, *A fractured twig.* An allusion to "A Twig Fell," a well-known poem by Chaim
Nachman Bialik (1873–1934), the "national poet" of the Hebrew Revival period.

Picture

The woods a flock of green sheep flowing down the hills
And the sea below splashed itself blue in the sun.
Clouds bloomed in the sky, floating like water lilies
And we were still little girls.

There was one among us with beloved eyes   5
And all of us envied her till we forgot.
And one was so fair and stood up so straight.
And when they called her in class, she could always reply.

And I'd go out in the sun to the nearby field
And love the clouds, spin stories about them all,   10
And I had plenty of time to ponder sorrow
From the first gray of autumn till the end of summer gold.

The Rending

He walked away, that stranger man,
Around his shoe a twist of vine,
A scarf was twined beneath his chin
And a mighty wind gored him.

Larks were whistling,   5
Starlings hung on a cloud
And the skies filled with the shriek of ravens,
Sunset terrors,
A lily-blaze.

And a wisp of straw, lifting in the wind,   10
Flashed and glinted like one of the stars.

*   *   *

Title, *The Rending* (Heb. *kri'ah*). Mourners' ritual tearing of their clothing at the
gravesite as an expression of grief.

Line 1, *stranger man* (Heb. *ha-ish ha-zar*). In Jewish lore, both the Messiah and the
dead are figured as wandering strangers.

Light and shade like clusters of grapes
Dangled black and green from a twig.

And a wisp of straw, lifting in the wind,
Twitched and was trapped between the ravens' wings.   15

He walked away, that stranger man,
Around his shoe a twist of vine,
A scarf was twined beneath his chin
And a mighty wind gored him.

The Sorrow of Night

The road so remote and steep,
The crescent moon like hammered tin,
And who can tell gold
From a bit of tin
No one would ever keep.   5

Clouds float steaming in the skies,
Dolorous roofs and towers rise,
And soaring on high, the foxes' cries
As their bodies writhe in the hedge.

Stars and planets, swarming bright,   10
Night falls into the Sea of Nights,
And leaping about like a doe, the light,
Like a fount gushing from a ledge.

A breaker claws the breasting waves,
Piercing the dread abyss headlong.   15
Lo, the sheaves stand upright in praise
And the reeds lift their voices in song:

*   *   *

Line 16, *the sheaves stand upright.* As in Joseph's dream, Gen. 37:7.

Return, O my soul, and rest thee
For the Lord thy God hath blest thee.

The road so remote and steep,   20
The crescent moon like hammered tin,
And above it a light
All milky-white
Streams like deliverance deep.

The Dove

Once there lived a pure white dove.
—That very dove ye must love.
Pinions she fashioned and flew far above.
—That very dove ye must love.

On the way she lit upon the Raven King.   5
—That very dove ye must love.
On her way she came upon wolves in a ring.
—That very dove ye must love.

Her foes she beheld, seventy strong.
—That very dove ye must love.   10
Those envious birds, they beat her ere long.
—That very dove ye must love.

Pure white she remained till she became prey.
—That very dove ye must love.
And a legend she is unto this very day.   15
—That very dove ye must love.

Lines 18–19, *Return, O my soul*. Psalm 116:7.

Sparks of Light

⸙

Sparks of Light

And this matter so dark is steeped in sparks of light
And their voice is not heard, not even a murmuring sound,
And they are like myrrh flowing from a flask all night.

And like perfumes they ooze, soft and serene they flow,
And in this matter so dark they gather to a bubbling fount 5
And in their comely delight they rise and overflow.

And in this matter so dark there opens a mine of gold
And this matter so dark reveals its depths profound
And tender is the love between the dark and the gold.

And in silence and peace they embrace, and no wind blows, 10
And the light keeps streaming and kissing the dark on the mouth
And the dark makes its body a well for the sparks of gold.

This matter so dark is steeped in sparks of light
And their voice is not heard, not even a murmuring sound,
And they are like myrrh flowing from a flask all night. 15

Title, *Sparks of Light* (Heb. *kitmey or*, lit. "color-patches of light"). The poem alludes to the Kabbalistic notion that sparks of divine light are trapped in fragments of the broken vessels of Creation, often found in the darkest of places.

"A little woman made the world"

A little woman made the world
Her bed,
That great round globe.
And it didn't escape the world
That a little woman   5
Lay resting on him.
And he grew grasses into her lap,
Wrapped her body
With leaves of grass.
Carried her off   10
As he carries mountains and valleys,
Lands and seas.
And this very woman would whisper:
O world—O bed of mine,
O world—rivers and streams,   15
Raging seas and even me.
Here I am, afloat like a sailor's daughter
And the world is my boat.
A swarm of stars like a swarm of bees
Humming around the globe.   20

The world cleaves to my belly,
My hands sprout up like flowers from the earth.
And atop that enormous globe,
Delight courses into my limbs.

A little woman made the world   25
Her bed
        —That great round globe.
And it didn't escape the world
        That a little woman
            Lay resting upon him.   30

Delight

There did I know a delight beyond all delight,
And it came to pass upon the Sabbath day
As tree boughs reached for the sky with all their might.

Round and round like a river streamed the light,
And the wheel of the eye craved the sunwheel that day.   5
Then did I know a delight beyond all delight.

The heads of the bushes blazed, insatiable bright
Sunlight striking the waves, igniting the spray.
It would swallow my head like a golden orange, that light.

Water lilies were gaping their yellow bright   10
Mouths to swallow the ripples and reeds in their way.
And indeed it came to pass on the Sabbath day
As tree boughs lusted for the sky with all their might,
And then did I know a delight beyond all delight.

Blue Lizard in the Sun

On a stone lay a blue-tailed lizard. Near at hand
The grasses seemed to her a forest grand
But the goodly sun no more than a grain of sand.

That goodly sun caresses her tail and head,
Thirst-quenching sun, like a festive table spread,   5
A golden ball the children coveted.

And her love reaches their bodies with fingers kind,
And her warmth hovers in the air like foam so fine,
And when she shines, how the backs of the lizards shine.

*   *   *

Line 9, *orange*. See "The Love of an Orange."

Title, *Blue Lizard in the Sun*. This parable is in the style of Ravikovitch's children's
verse.

At her gaze they grow gold and red and blue on the ground.   *10*
When she shines for them between the trees' great crowns
They see the sap ooze, they see the leaves go brown.

The great trees turn their faces, shamed and stunned,
And the grasses crowd to the breast of the earth as one,
But the lizards alone keep nuzzling that warm sun.   *15*

On a stone lay a blue-tailed lizard. Near at hand
The grasses seemed to her a forest grand
But the goodly sun shrank like a grain of sand.

Love

Two fishes raced the waves,
Down to the ocean deep
So each to each could tell
How great the depth of their love.

Two fishes, they would dive   *5*
And dally in the ocean deep,
And the farther they did go
The deeper was their love.

Nevermore did they venture above,
These lovers of the ocean deep.   *10*
No tongue can ever tell
How great the depth of their love.

Intoxication

If only I had the red dress that eludes me still,
That dress of great price,
And if only I had a young hart leaping upon the hills,
Bounding upon the heights—

From the rooftops we would swing   5
And the wings of the winds we'd bind
Until they were all entangled
Like a braid of twine.

The winds would puff their cheeks and take flight
Till the sun went forth like a strongman,   10
Swaggering in his might.

From his table he'd throw me crumbs
That would blaze upon the red dress,
And lowing, assail me again,
Goring me with hornèd rays   15
Like oxen twain.

And the leaves of the bushes would murmur and chime
Like showering coins of gold,
And he'd gaze at me in love, he'd gaze enthralled,
And I'd call: 20

Be thou like a young hart, O beloved mine.

Lines 3–4, *leaping . . . Bounding.* Song of Songs 2:8.

Line 10, *Till the sun went forth.* Cf. Judges 5:31, "as the sun when he goeth forth in his might," and Psalm 19:4–5, "the sun . . . rejoiceth like a strong man to run a race."

Line 14, *assail* (Heb. *histolel,* a hapax), Exod. 9:17.

Line 21, *a young hart.* Song of Songs 2:9, 8:14.

The Seasons of the Year

༺༻

The Seasons of the Year

I

Through the outliers the winds do blow,
The scent of spices waft away,
As seasons and feast days come and go.

The tree sheds his leaves in the cold,
The cloud lets his tresses grow   5
And tucks away his molten gold.

A gloomy dark creeps up from the land
And turns the rivers deep and bold
As eight candles light the lamp.

No light save for that drop of glow,   10
No heat in the land save for that flame.
How but in lamps shall splendor grow?

Through the outliers the winds do blow,
The scent of spices waft away
As seasons and feast days come and go.   15

Line 1, *outliers* (Heb. *charigim*). A neologistic use of the root *ch.r.g*, denoting deviation, eccentricity, or detachment from a center.

Line 10, *drop of glow*. A Kabbalistic image; see "Sparks of Light."

An azure quiet as milk in the bowl,
And the light revels in what he's wrought
And the cold silver turns to gold.

The soil on the hill like copper-rust,
And branches of trees, red in the sun,   20
Inhale the sunheat in their lust.

The whistling reeds sway to and fro,
The leaves grow round and green again,
The rivers tremble and gently flow.

Summer and winter, spring and fall,   25
Wide open sea and rivers all,
Mountain and forest, flower and bush,
Limber grasses green and lush,
The wand'ring light like a prince enthralled,
The chill of silver, the heat of gold,   30
Turn round and round in the wheel of the year,
Drift on and on in the seasons of the year,
Along with you in the seasons of the year.

II

There's a light that's blue and an amber sea,
A day one sees all things entwine,   35
A lake one sees, winds roist'ring free,
Trains like gazelles racing by,
And fanning out, landmass and bay,
Gigantic slabs fissured away.
There's a man I knew, and whence he came   40
And what befell him, and I knew his name
    —Then shall the world turn as seagulls dive
        And the olive tree become a vine—

There is a man, real as can be,
Who moves among them like a stream in the sea.   45
And cities and sands and roads as they run
All lusting after the wanton sun.

*   *   *

Line 47, *lusting after.* Recalling Gen. 3:16, the woman's desire for her husband.

And kittens and dogs leap over the gate,
Skip this way and that for a scrap to eat.

And seagulls whip up the frothing sea   50

And joy keeps climbing hand over hand.

And were there among them a beloved man
Like the oryx horn may his glory be.

Around Jerusalem

There is a train that goes round
And around Jerusalem
At night.

Birds there circle far above her,
Beat their wings, and with a clamor   5
In the dark they shed a feather
On the Jebus threshing floor.

Black trees stand beside the track,
The tunnel calls the burrow black.
There's a sheen of polished rock   10
In the dry creek at her back.

*   *   *

Line 53, *oryx* (Heb. *re'em*). Deut. 33:17, from Moses's blessing for Joseph. Cf. Psalm 92:10.

Title, *Around Jerusalem*. Psalm 125:2, lit. "Jerusalem, mountains around her, and the Lord is around his people." Jerusalem is personified as female throughout the Bible.

Line 7, *Jebus threshing floor*. The Jebusites were a Canaanite people whose territory, Jebus, was to become the site of Jerusalem (1 Chron. 11:4). The threshing floor where David built an altar is identified as the future site of Solomon's Temple (1 Chron. 21:18–22:1).

At night there's a train
That goes round
And around Jerusalem.

Mountains circle round about her,   15
Winds make moan from ruins inside her.
Birds are screeching in the calm air
And when night falls, owl eyes glimmer.

Mountains hang upon her breast
Like a crown, a regal vest.   20
A golem's clawing at her dust,
Growling like a hunted beast.

A clatter in the heart of dark,
In the gloomy hell pit. Hark:
A golem growling Hallelujah.   25

The Moon in the Rain

See the moon on the lowly mud.
She shines on the sides of the road,
On the cypress tall
And the swarm below
Whose life so bare   5
Counts for less than a hair.

* * *

Line 24, *gloomy hell pit* (Heb. *ma'apelya*, a hapax). Jer. 2:31, "a land of dark despair"
(Anchor Bible).

Title, *Moon* (Heb. *levana*, fem.). The literary term for moon, as distinguished from the
common term *yare'ach*, masc.; see "Waning and Waxing."

Line 1, *the lowly mud*. In Jewish mysticism, the sparks of divine light can often be
recovered from the humblest of places; see "Sparks of Light."

Over the backs bent low,
Over the heads raised high,
On those who fly
The tempest's blight
Her light will grow
Like mushrooms overnight.

10

Like the Rolling Dust before the Whirlwind

Kislev and Nisan, like horses twain,
Gallop around the zodiac wheel.
In the moon of Tammuz the wind roars,
Flogging the tree with knotted whips.
No longer do lions scold in the night,
No angels sing their chants at night.
Like a seething cauldron the wind roars.
There's a god hiding behind the rain.

5

Deep in the mountain embers flare;
Like the sides of a pot the night is charred.
In the month to come, you will waft us aloft
In a swift and beautiful sailing craft
On the Great Sea from shore to shore.
The radiant face of the sea will flood
And in its cunning, the stricken tree
Will flower at dawn in a burst of red.
How bitter it is when the wind roars!

10

15

❖   ✳   ❖

Title and line 21, *Like the Rolling Dust . . . like chaff.* Isa. 17:13: "God shall rebuke them, and they shall flee far off, . . . like the chaff of the mountains before the wind, and like a rolling thing before the whirlwind."

Lines 1–3, *Kislev . . . Nisan . . . Tammuz.* Months in the Hebrew lunar calendar, associated with the ancient Near Eastern zodiac, falling between November–December, March–April, and June–July.

Lines 8, 23, *a god hiding* (Heb. *el mistater*). Also a reference to El, the ancient Near Eastern deity.

In the moon of Tammuz the tree moans
When the wind flogs it with knotted whips.
The moon of Nisan slips away like a thief,   20
The moon of Kislev like chaff in the wind.
Like a seething cauldron the wind roars.
There's a god hiding behind the rain.

HARD
WINTER

for Yitzhak

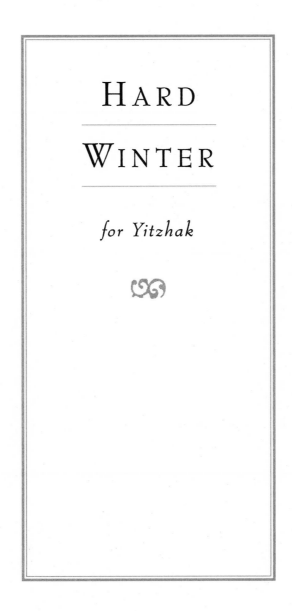

Questions and Answers

And when our youth ends? I asked.
And when our youth ends, they replied.
Indeed, they're like all those diviners of yore;
By now many have sailed for old age.
If our youth ends, so what? they asked.   *5*

And when our youth ends, I said,
And when our youth ends, I raged,
Fantastical monsters shall rise from the seas
And a drought descend upon the land.
Perverse shall be our youth when it ends.   *10*

And when our youth ends, they scoffed,
Like the hornet's flight our youth shall end,
Or else like the flower of late-blooming roses
That once could waken beauty and love.
Still in our lifetime our youth shall end.   *15*

And when our youth ends? I asked.
If our youth ends, this time I reply,
The warm waters of the Great Sea
Shall dry like mist if our youth ends
And the ocean seethe with beasts of the deep.   *20*

Title, *Questions and Answers*. The form of this poem reflects the Responsa, a genre of rabbinic literature in which learned authorities responded in writing to questions about Jewish law as it applied to everyday life.

The Blue West

Time Caught in a Net

And again I was like one of those little girls,
Fingernails black with toil,
Building tunnels in the sand.
Wherever my eye rested, ribbons of purple.
And many eyes shining like silver beads.   5
Again I was like one of those little girls
Who sail around the whole world in one night,
All the way to the land of Cathay
And Madagascar,
And those who break cups and saucers   10
From so much love,
So much love,
So much love.

Faraway Land

Tonight I returned in a sailing boat
From the isles of the sun, the coral reefs.
Girls with combs of gold in their hair
Remained onshore in the isles of the sun.

Four whole years of honey and milk 5
I roamed the shore on the isles of the sun.
The market stands were laden with fruit,
The cherries lay gleaming there in the sun.

Sailors and skippers from seventy lands
Went sailing off to the isles of the sun. 10
Four whole years in that radiant light
I kept on counting ships of gold.

Four whole years round as an apple,
I kept on stringing coral beads.
Merchants and mongers on the isles of the sun 15
Were spreading out their crimson silks.

And the sea was deeper than any depth
When I returned from the isles of the sun.
Heavy as honey, the drops of sun
Trickled on the island when the sun went down. 20

Murmurings

And they twitter with a fluting voice
From break of day till thick of night,
From flower nodes to forest deep,
Until the forest is born from the gloom.

And they twitter with a rilling voice, 5
Over the torches of the burning sun,
From the going forth of the burning sun
As it leaves its chamber for the lands of the North.

And they twitter with a murmuring voice,
Suspended soaring in the gyres of sky, 10

Line 7, *the going forth of the . . . sun.* Psalm 19:4–6.

They twitter with a voice that startles the sun
From its chamber deep in the thick of night.

And they rescue the forest from the gloomy dark,
And they are the ones that count the sparks,
And they are the ones that count the weeks   *15*
And the years among the blades of grass.

And they recount the rapture of days
Even when I am still asleep.

Hills of Salt

Sea foam fluttered like the wings of birds
And two salt hills were left on the beach,
And all the sea long it was lake upon lake,
And sailboats tiny as a thumb,
Their colors like bubbles of soap.   *5*

And the two of us sat, each by his lakes,
Two strips of beach between us
And a wealth of seaweed.
And the heavy fronds swayed in and out,
Clinging to the teeth of the reefs, soughing unbridled lust. *10*

A mass of seaweed broke loose and fell at my feet
And my eyelids were heavy with light.
And the sea rose up and spilled from pool to pool,
And on its blue streams there lay a sheet of gleam.

Lakes were brimming in the palms of our hands,   *15*
The strips of beach between us—two arms wide.
And we didn't draw near all that day, not by a hair,
Our bodies like two hills of salt, our feet like seaweed.

Line 14, *sparks*. As in the Kabbalistic story of Creation; see "Sparks of Light."

The Hurling

When the bells tolled and the muezzin wailed
And the rooster railed against the moon,
A great hurling gripped Jerusalem
And the King's palace lit up the streets.

In King Solomon's stables   5
Monkeys and parrots were screeching,
A gift to him from Tahpenes the Queen
By the hand of merchants
And highwaymen.

The waters of Shiloah gathered to a growling cataract   10
And fell upon the Valley of Hinnom.
Its rivulets tore their hearts out
In the clefts of the rock.
In King Solomon's stables
Princes labored like hirelings,   15
Ready to harness the royal chariot
At the pleasure of the King.

     *   *   *

Title, *The Hurling*. Isa. 22:17–18, lit. "Behold, the Lord will hurl you away . . . ; there you will die." See "Hovering at a Low Altitude," line 59.

Line 1, *muezzin*. One who calls Muslims to prayer from the minaret of a mosque. Here and in lines 18–19, Ravikovitch provides a contemporary Israeli frame for her biblical prophecy of doom.

Line 7, *Tahpenes*. An Egyptian queen (1 Kings 11:19–20). Also, the name of an ancient Egyptian city: "At Tehaphnehes, also, the day shall be darkened, when I shall break there the yokes of Egypt; . . . a cloud shall cover her, and her daughters shall go into captivity" (Ezek. 30:18). Ravikovitch is projecting this prophecy of Egypt's doom onto Jerusalem. Cf. also Jer. 43:7–9.

Line 10, *Shiloah*. Inverting Isa. 8:6, "the waters of Shiloah, that go softly."

Line 11, *Valley of Hinnom* (Heb. *gey-ben-hinom*). A valley south of Jerusalem, the scene of pagan rites, including child sacrifices (Jer. 7:31, 2 Kings 23:10); *gehinom*, Gehenna in English, later came to denote hell.

When the bells tolled and the muezzin wailed,
Two border guards took to their beds
With curses on their lips.   *20*
On a cloud black as a Cushite's hand
Jerusalem the City of David was hurled away
Like a finger lopped from the body.

Flowers of Every Color

I was told to bring flowers of every color
And whatever time despoiled,
And a night when the moon is whole
As new coins from the Emperor's mint
Whose form was not defaced.   *5*
(And our hearts were quickened
For their form was not defiled.)
I was told to bring bars of unformed clay,
The love of the Philistine captains,
A Dagon struck down on the steps of their temple,   *10*
A baby dying in the palms of Baal-Zebub,
And those who've gone down to the dust
And send up a glimmer from among the dead.

I was told to bring whatever I could find,
The leftover spoils of every baited trap.   *15*

Line 10, *Dagon*. A national deity of the ancient Philistines, represented as a fish-tailed man; cf. 1 Sam. 5:2–4, "the head of Dagon and both the palms of his hands were cut off upon the threshold."

Line 11, *Baal-Zebub* (Heb. *Ba'al-Zevuv*, "Lord of the Flies"). A Philistine deity; cf. 2 Kings 1:2.

Line 15, *baited trap* (Heb. *pechatim*, a hapax). 2 Sam. 17:9.

The Blue West

If there was nothing but a road there,
The ruins of some workshops,
One fallen minaret
And a few carcasses of machines,
Why couldn't I   5
Come into the heart of the field?
There is nothing more painful
Than a field
With a stone weighing on its heart.

I want to reach beyond that hill,   10
Want to reach,
Want to come.
I want to break out of the depths of the earth,
From the soles of my feet even unto my head—
The depths of the earth.   15
I want to reach the ends of thought
Whose very beginnings
Slash like a knife.
I want to ascend to the fringes of the sun
And not fall prey to the fire.   20

If one could only walk about
With grasshopper feet on the water,
If one could only ascend
The great arch of the sun's rays,
If one could only reach   25
All the cities beyond the sea—
And here is another painful sight:
A seashore that has no ships.

*   *   *

Line 14, *soles . . . head.* Isa. 1:6.

Line 20, *fall prey to the fire* (Heb. *ma'akholet esh*). A rare biblical portmanteau (Isa.
9:5, 19) combining the sense of "fuel of fire" with *ma'akhelet*, a ritual slaughtering
knife (Gen. 22:6).

On one of the days in the year to come
The eye of the sea will grow dark 30
With a multitude of ships.
Then shall the very depths of the earth
Be stretched on high like a tent-cloth.
And a sun will shine for us blue as the sea,
A sun will shine for us warm as an eye, 35
Will wait for us till we ascend
As it heads for the blue west.

Line 30, *eye of the sea* (Heb. *eyn ha-yam*). Also "color/appearance of the sea."

Line 33, *tent-cloth*. Psalm 104:2, "stretching out heavens like a tent-cloth" (Alter, *Psalms*).

Warm Memories

Requiem after Seventeen Years

The cantor was reading psalms.
The trees whispered like a flock of black priests.
We were not much taller than the gravestones
And we knew there would be no resurrection in our day.
At a distance, there stood a ladder   5
For the ascent of the holy and pure, who are as the very sapphire
(Most of them lay at our feet),
And our lives were like a locust at the border of sun and shade.
But when the drowned girl passed through all the chambers of the sea,
We knew it is the sea that fathers the rivers.   10

Line 6, *the holy and pure*. From the funeral prayer, *El Maleh Rachamim* ("O God Full of Mercy"): "Grant . . . perfect rest beneath the shadow of thy divine presence, in the exalted places among the holy and pure, who shine as the brightness of the firmament." See "Finally I'm Talking."

Mahlon and Chilion

What, he thought, is this wondrous thing?
If it seizes me, this wondrous thing,
Like a viper on black turbid waters
My day will darken, I'll be dead.

If it seizes me, this wondrous thing,   5
Loosener of limbs on turbid waters,
On the seven seas will I be diffused,
Floating to that wondrous place.

What, he thought, is this wondrous thing?
Hollows of light on turbid waters,   10
Vipers that live in the wilderness
Stifle a moan like me, like me.

And what, he thought, is this wondrous thing?
This wondrous thing has stricken me now,
My head twitters like a bird, it blooms,   15
I rejoice and die like a fool.

Title, *Mahlon and Chilion.* The two sons of Naomi who died in the land of Moab
(Ruth 1:2); their names, "Sickness" and "Annihilation," foreshadow their fate.

Line 6, *Loosener of limbs* (Heb. *ednat evarim,* lit. "pleasure of limbs"; the noun *edna*
suggests sexual pleasure, Gen. 18:12). Lines 6–7 may recall Sappho's description of
Eros: "Irresistible / and bittersweet / / that loosener / of limbs, Love / / reptile-like /
strikes me down" (Fragment 130, trans. Mary Barnard).

Line 15, *twitters . . . blooms.* The first verb, *metsayets,* can mean both "twitter" and
"bud"; the second, *pore'ach,* can mean both "bloom" and "fly." A direct quote from
Yehuda Amichai's quatrain about the spilled blood of a dying soldier, "In a Right
Angle," #45; cf. also Num. 17:8, the flowering of Aaron's rod.

Trying

Remember you promised to come on the holiday
One hour after dark.
I've left debts in a number of places,
Would you care to settle them?
Since you'll be coming after dark   5
No one will notice you.
Since you'll be coming after dark
I will notice you.

Hard to understand why the heater
Burns and burns, yet the house   10
Does not grow warm.
I feel as if the walls of the house
Are writhing with pain inside the plaster,
And yet we keep postponing it all
From day to day till the end of days.   15
What a fraud: to act as if we
Were children of the gods.

Remember you promised to come on the holiday
One hour after dark.
For my part, I won't keep count of wraths   20
Or wrongs till you come.
And you: Don't believe a word I say
Even when it's wondrous or perverse.

I lie down to sleep like ordinary mortals
And I don't practice magic.   25
I forgo the honors in advance,
I bear no resemblance to the daughters of the gods.
And you: Remember when and where.

The Second Trying

If I could only get hold of the whole of you,
How could I ever get hold of the whole of you,
Even more than the most beloved idols,
More than mountains quarried whole,
     More than mines   *5*
      Of burning coal,
Let's say mines of extinguished coal
And the breath of day like a fiery furnace.

If one could get hold of you for all the years,
How could one get hold of you from all the years,   *10*
How could one lengthen a single arm,
Like a single branch of an African river,
As one sees in a dream the Bay of Storms,
As one sees in a dream a ship that went down,
The way one imagines a cushion of clouds,   *15*
Lily-clouds as the body's cushion,
But though you will it, they will not convey you,
Do not believe that they will convey you.

If one could get hold of all-of-the-whole-of-you,
If one could get hold of you like metal,   *20*
Say like pillars of copper,
Say like a pillar of purple copper
(That pillar I remembered last summer)—
And the bottom of the ocean I have never seen,
And the bottom of the ocean that I can see   *25*
With its thousand heavy thickets of air,
A thousand and one laden breaths.

If one could only get hold of the-whole-of-you-now,
How could you ever be for me what I myself am?

Line 29, *be for me*. Inverting *Pirkey Avot* (Ethics of the Fathers) 1:14: "[Hillel] used to say: If I am not for myself, who will be for me? And being for my own self, what am I?"

Tirzah's Dreams

Tell him right now
All of my love,
Two hours before dawn
Tell it all.
Don't waste your breath on saying hello,   5
Until break of day, tell him
My love.

I saw a house that had weather vanes,
I saw a garden filled with treetops,
My love devoured them,   10
My love in all the trees.

Confound his dreams,
Tell him only my love,
Don't waste your time to no avail,
Most words aren't real.   15
Brew him a potion when he awakes,
Not as a mere mortal will he awake;
Tell him only my love
Until his dreams stammer,
Don't waste your breath on courtesies   20
Two hours before dawn.

Bring him to the courtyard,
Bring him to the laurels,
As if potion-drunk he will come and dream,
All of my love will he dream.   25

Beloved mine, beloved mine:
All of my love
I could not tell.

Title, *Tirzah*. Hebrew name, feminine form of the root "desire"; biblical symbol of beauty, cf. Song of Songs 6:4; one of Ravikovitch's poetic personae.

Warm Memories

Imagine: Only the dust was at my side,
I had no other companion.
Dust walked me to nursery school,
Ruffled my hair
On the warmest childhood days.   5

Imagine who was at my side
And all the girls had another.
When winter started slinging its terrible nets,
When the clouds devoured their prey,
Imagine who was at my side   10
And how much I wanted another.

The pinecones rattled, and for a while
I ached to be alone with the wind.
Many a night I'd dream in a daze
Of a few lone houses moist with love.   15
Imagine how deprived I was
If the dust was my only companion.

On the hamsin days, I'd sail all the way
To the capital city of the great whales.
I was filled with a reckless happiness.   20
I'd never come back till the day I died,

But when I came back, I was like a raven
Despised by its raven cousins.
I had no companion at all,
And only the dust was at my side.   25

Line 18, *hamsin*. Dry hot weather caused by desert winds from the south.

The Roar of the Waters

꩜

The Roar of the Waters

A bird twittered like a madwoman
Until it was spent
And then it wept.
I sank in a cloud of tenderness,
I sank   5
I dissolved.
But no, I was drowned in the ocean,
There a man loved me
Didn't leave me a fingernail.
His hand grasped my hair,   10
In the hammering ocean
I was set to be wrecked.
His hand pulled at my hair
In the swarms of the ocean
I no longer remember a thing.   15

Title, *The Roar of the Waters.* Isa. 17:12–13 (lit. "a roaring like the roaring of many waters"), Jer. 51:55, Psalm 65:7.

Line 12, *set to be wrecked.* Jonah 1:4, "the ship was like to be broken."

A Hard Winter

The little berry danced in the flame
And before its glory set, it was lapped in gloom.
Rain and sun ruled by turns, in the house
We shuddered to think what would become of us.
The bushes reddened at their hearts   5
And the pond hid away;
Each one attended to himself alone.
But for a moment my attention wandered
And I saw how people are cut down in this world—
As when lightning strikes a tree   10
Laden with limbs and living tissue,
So are their wet branches trampled like dead grass.
The shutter was damaged, the walls thin.
Rain and sun, by turns, rode past on iron wheels.
The plants, flesh and sinew, were intent on themselves alone.   15
This time I never thought I'd survive.

Heartbreak in the Park

In radiant Hyde Park
Facing the warm stone gate,
Old men and a multitude of mothers
Glided by without touching.
Pupils who sneaked out of class   5
Were taunting the ducks in the water.
A dog burst into the lake
And the assembly of ducks took flight, insulted.

Line 6, *the pond hid away* (Heb. *ha-brekha nechbe'a*). An allusion to "The Pond," an influential poem by Chaim Nachman Bialik (1873–1934), the "national poet" of the Hebrew Revival period.

Line 12, *trampled* (Heb. *hayu le-mirmas,* Isa. 5:5). Calling into question the notion of divine justice in the parable of the vineyard.

Old men reposed on their canvas chairs.
And I set my heart to learn: 10
He who departs for an hour is as good as gone forever.

Across the way, the scent of vanilla
Wafted out of the genteel café.
Nice husbands collected the coats of their wives.
A student from the provinces stretched out on the grass,   15
Fixed his gaze on the sky and fingered the clouds.
Colorful crowds flounced up and down the steps,
Busses waddled by like a herd of red elephants.

All these broke my heart,
Words failed me.   20
I knew I had the right to roam without rebuke.
Not far away was another garden with its boats
And all its chirping and chirring.

I didn't realize at the time
What a pang my heart sustained in the heat.   25
I thought about the roses, how orange they were.
There was nothing more beautiful than the roses.
In the gaps of the meager hedge, the heat crouched like a vampire.
All of it utterly broke my heart,
It broke my heart.   30
Soon I dissolved like the drone of a wasp as it buzzes past.

Crane

I shall come to him early tomorrow,
May the would-be wise shrivel like bitter gourds,
And the meddlers, may their lips be lashed,
Thus will it be at that early hour.

*   *   *

Line 2, *bitter gourds* (Heb. *paku'ot*, a hapax). 2 Kings 4:39, considered a deadly
poison.

Thus do I wish to come to him tomorrow,   5
When my dreams are all aflow with longings,
When my dreams will all be rid of their thorns
And not fade away at the usual hour.

Perchance he will be standing at my side.
Then might I soar over him like plumage,   10
Then might I shine like the peacock's tail.

He's the one who always ends up above,
He's the one who blights me with love,
He's like a bird that never will be snared.

Tirzah and the Whole Wide World

Carry me off to the ends of the North,
Carry me to the Atlantic Ocean.
Set me with folk of another kind
The likes of whom I have never met.
I'll eat wild blackberries baked in a pie   5
And race in a train across Scandinavia.

Carry me to the Pacific Ocean,
Set me among the tawny fishes,
Among dolphins, salmon and snark,
Among kingfishers dozing on the mast.   10
I shall not be in the least surprised
When you bring me to meet the great Atlantic.

Bring me unto the weeping rivers,
Those desolate shores wasting away,
Where kangaroo pursues kangaroo,   15
Both sporting a coat of many colors.
Bring me unto the kangaroo,
Set me down in the forest damp.

      *   *   *

Wait for me in the belly of the ship,
Ready the high-speed train for me.   20
I shall come soon, I shall not tarry,
To dwell among nations of another kind.
Among those strangers I shall grin
As salmon do, deep in the sea.
If you cannot get me an ocean,   25
Get me mountains with an icing of snow.

Among Christian mariners set me down,
Bring me to old Norway's shore.
Bring me to Australia's desert,
The most forlorn desert of all.   30
I shall instruct the kangaroo
In Hebrew Bible and the three Rs.
Please do let the strangers know
I shall come to them presently.

Let them know: In the year to come   35
I shall be at the heart of the ocean.
Tell them now to ready the nets
To fish up ring after ring for me.

Magic Spells

Today I'm a hill,
Tomorrow a sea.
Wandering all day
Like Miriam's well,
A bubble astray   5
In a crannied wall.

*   *   *

Line 4, *Miriam's well*. According to rabbinic legend, a miraculous well that followed
the Israelites during their forty years of wandering in the desert.

At night in my bed
I dreamt horses red,
Purple and green,

In the morning I heard   10
A babble of water,
The parrots' yatter.

Today I'm a snail,
Tomorrow a tree
Tall as a palm.   15

A nook yesterday,
A seashell today.
Tomorrow I'm tomorrow.

Scoffing

Little Mount Lebanon keeps eroding away,
And the rose of Sharon, the lily of the valley.
Giants bar the waters of a creek with their spears
Though such scoffing is surely a crime.
Only giants would heap dust on something that shudders like a vein.   5
The water passes through a ditch in the shadow of cedars
And there are pine trees too, shrubs and slugs of every kind.
The creek is quite willing to disappear
But it goes on shimmering as it flickers out.
Little Mount Lebanon keeps eroding away   10
And the lily of the valley too.

Title and lines 4–5, *Scoffing . . . heap dust*. Inverting Hab. 1:10, "And they shall scoff at
the kings, and the princes shall be a scorn unto them; . . . for they shall heap dust."

Line 1, *Mount Lebanon*. Mountain range in Lebanon, source of the famed cedars used
in building Solomon's Temple (1 Kings 5:5–10).

Line 2, *rose of Sharon, the lily of the valley*. Song of Songs 2:1.

Outrage

In that place,
In one of those places,
Flowers were savagely rent asunder,
Flowers were devoured like prey.
Dogs gnashed their teeth at them,   5
Dogs howled in their savage hour.
Flowers were savagely rent asunder.
Oh God,
The beauty in that place!

In that place,   10
Set apart from all such places,
Like sunflowers did they seem,
Sunflowers counting the steps of the sun.
When they lifted their heads on high
Their scent ascended the steps of the sun.   15
And many hours after that rending,
And hours even after they died,
That burning soul of theirs still shone.
Oh God,
The outrage in that place!   20

Title, *Outrage*. The Hebrew title, *oshek*, is a biblical term of outrage at the violent oppression and robbing of the underprivileged, as in Prov. 22:16.

Line 3, *savagely*. I.e., with violent injustice; with rage. The Hebrew alludes to Jer. 22:3 (NRSV): "Act with justice and righteousness, and deliver from the hand of the oppressor anyone who has been robbed. And do no wrong or violence to the alien, the orphan, and the widow, or shed innocent blood in this place."

Line 16, *rending* (Heb. *kri'a*). Literalizing the symbolic act of tearing one's clothing at the gravesite as an expression of grief. See "The Rending."

Unclear Days

༄༅

War in Zanzibar

During the years of that lawless war,
An agent set out on a secret mission
For Zanzibar in Africa.
To this day his carcass has not been found.

During those days, a few young men   5
Would fasten their eyes upon the sky,
Would squint their eyes, straining to see
If a parachute dropped in the heart of the jungle.

Two long weeks, in the heart of the jungle,
They fastened their eyes upon the heavens.   10
Like rain stuck in the gut of the sky
No parachute dropped in all of Zanzibar.

Midnights a skull would float along,
The face of the moon like a drifting carcass.
Although he had a will of steel   15
That man never made it to Zanzibar.

*   *   *

Title, *War in Zanzibar*. A poem written in the context of large-scale Israeli military aid and training in Africa prior to the 1967 war.

Line 13, *a skull would float*. See *Pirkey Avot* (Ethics of the Fathers) 2:7: "Moreover, he saw a skull floating on the surface of the water. He said to it, Because thou drownedst others, they have drowned thee."

Inside the stifling straw-hut air,
Young men were scratching their white skin.
In Zanzibar, in a stubble field,
Their day suddenly went dark. 20

The End of the War

He came at midnight, both legs lopped off,
Though his old wounds had long since healed.
He came through the third-story window—
I was struck with wonder at how he got in.
We'd lived through an age of calamity; 5
Many had lost their closest kin.
In streets sown with shredded papers
The orphan survivors were skipping about.

I was frozen as crystal when he came.
He thawed me like pliant wax, 10
Altered me even as the pall of night
Turns into the feather of dawn.
His bold spirit translucent as mist
That streams from the morning clouds.

Line 2, *healed* (Heb. *karmu or*, lit. "formed a skin"). Ezek. 37:6, 8, from his prophecy
of the resurrection of the dry bones.

Line 8, *survivors* (Heb. *she'erit ha-pleta*, "the surviving remnant"). A common term for
Holocaust survivors.

Line 11, *pall* (Heb. *etun*, a hapax), Prov. 7:16.

On Account of a King

The great army conquered the sea,
Its flank pressed heavy onto Sidon.
Greek isles groaned under its loins;
The orphans of Galilee sobbed.

Hulking soldiers in fetid rags   5
Crowded into the coastal markets.
The market women recoiled in fright
But the elders kept fawning on them.

The towering soldiers, sore beset,
Had to barter with colored stones.   10
Even in the cobbled city square
Their eyes seemed to gather moss.

They'd whisper into each others' ears,
The hawkers all convulsed with laughter:
The great Emperor, Lord of the Troops,   15
Hath neither sword nor spear!

In the dark corners of the marketplace
The youths of Sidon huddled with their lords,
Creeping about in cliques and cabals
To snatch at the reins of power.   20

The great army never stirred from its tents,
Shadows leaned over lances all night.
They had no leisure, those thickset men,
To dally where the beds are soft.

But the eyes of the youths glittered like coins,   25
The hawkers brazenly stashed their gains.
Dimmed were all the centurions' eyes
For their king had neither sword nor spear.

Line 2, *flank . . . onto Sidon.* Gen. 49:13, "his flank upon Sidon" (Alter, *Five Books of Moses*). Poem may be loosely based on the conquest of Sidon (in today's Lebanon) by the Roman general Pompey the Great in 64 B.C.E.

The Turning of the Times

As he cleaved to his copybook, fifteen years,
A ring of mildew blackened his head,
A fat thorn poked from the paving stones
And the cats had their litter of kittens each year
(The little ones quickly scampered to the eaves). 5
Sea tides seethed as night declined,
Mornings the world was set to be wrecked.
Well versed was he in the seasons' wrath
(Winter's wounds would soften in spring).
Rumors of earthquakes reached his ear 10
And the frequent natural disasters too.
The roar of the waters he did not forget,
For the victims of slaughter he would weep.
And yet at times he'd see, to his joy,
A moon grown portly as a tub. 15
But once in his life he chanced to see
How a mighty wind blows seed about,
Blows seed about, time out of mind.

The Further Travels of the Sea-Wolf

Before dawn
A plane crashed in the vacant lot;
Apart from the pilot who was killed
There were no passengers on board.
Suddenly the plane opened its jaws 5
Like the gullet of a fleeing fish.
How astounded I was to see
That its wings were lopped off.

Line 7, *set to be wrecked*. Jonah 1:4, "the ship was like to be broken." Lines 7 and 12, see "The Roar of the Waters."

Title, *the Sea-Wolf*. A large marine fish; also alluding to Jack London's 1903 novel about Wolf Larsen, a sea captain.

Then its belly became distended
And the groin folds of the metal seethed.   *10*
If it sought to fly again
It would surely be scorned.
And yet the sea-wolf goes on fleeing
From his brother's ship, the *Macedonia*.
He sails on in a tissue of mists   *15*
Ten cubits across the seas.
He doesn't see the red of the sun,
Even the storms have let him be.
My mind cannot abide
That he should come to an end.   *20*

Unclear Days

One day it happened that a soldier was killed
On the brick facade of a makeshift shed
At the gate of an orchard with its weepy faucet.
On one of the frightening unclear days
That fall between Tishrey and Cheshvan.   *5*

Someone believes he killed that soldier,
Killed him unwittingly, or so he thinks.
In the unclear years that follow that day,
There are those who doubt he was killed at all.
Gazelles abound in the mountain clefts.   *10*
Was there anyone else in the olive grove?

Lunacy bounds in his head like a hare,
He ruminates madly on the olive grove.
Before he sleeps he will sometimes glimpse
A man pacing at the windowsill.   *15*

*   *   *

Line 14, *Macedonia*. The ship of Wolf Larsen's brother; cf. chapters 24–25.

Lines 4–5, *unclear days . . . Tishrey and Cheshvan*. First two months of the Jewish year, beginning with the Days of Awe from Rosh Hashana to Yom Kippur, when it is still undetermined whether one is to be reinscribed in the Book of Life.

The road is paved, the house stands firm,
And only gazelles live in those hills.
But during the unclear days of Cheshvan
The grove fills with my swarming fears.
A man appears in Mandate gear;   20
A lad attends him, lending a hand.

He draws near the low window, so it seems,
But why is that man in such a rush?
If he tries to plunge his dagger in me
—perhaps some vile thing was done to him—   25
I will evade him for a little while
Until the new age drives him away.

Shunra

Shunra was pink and white as a delectable cake.
She'd been to London, she'd been to Moscow too,
All her days were like a Sabbath
Under a cloud, but her garden flowered more each day.
When the rain came down, the glass roof of the house would leak.   5
She drew near the window where someone awaited her.
He was reading a letter but she addled his brain.
He set down the letter and kissed her like a delectable cake.
All this came to pass rather late in the morning
And he kept smacking his lips all day long, all day long.   10
Shunra spread a napkin on her lap and licked away at a vanilla cake.

Line 20, *Mandate gear*. In the colonial style, e.g., khaki shorts and knee socks, commonly worn during the period of British rule over Palestine (1918–1948).

Line 25, *vile thing*. Judges 19:24, the story of the murder of the Levite's concubine.

Title, *Shunra*. After the Aramaic for "cat"; one of Ravikovitch's poetic personae. The *shunra* appears in a different context in the familiar Passover song *Chad Gadya*.

Shunra II

Shunra set out to splash about in a puddle of golden water.
Peasants in their helmets were toiling in the castle fields.
The Duke's son set a special sentry over Shunra;
Under his helmet's visor, the sentry's eyes grew dark.
Shrubbery shadows fell across the water and the reeds lay low,   5
Shrubbery flecks reached Shunra as they faded away.
Shunra closed her eyes in the quiet puddle.
She may have dozed off for a while, but Shunra doesn't drown.

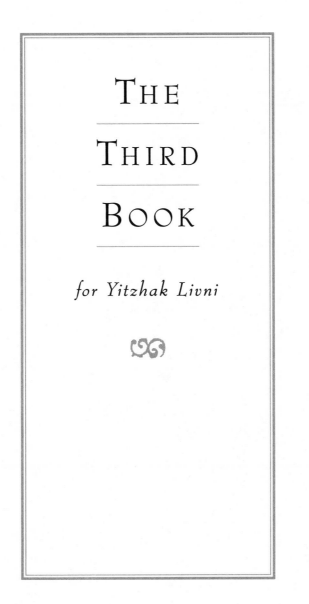

THE
THIRD
BOOK

for Yitzhak Livni

Surely You Remember

After they all go home
I remain alone with the poems,
some of my own,
some of others.
Poems that others have written I love best of all.   5
I remain in the silence
and the choking in my throat relaxes.
I remain.
Sometimes I wish they would all go home.
Writing poems may be a pleasant thing to do.   10
You sit in your room and the walls grow taller.
Colors grow bolder.
A blue kerchief turns into the depth of a well.
You wish everyone would leave.
You don't know what's the matter with you.   15
Perhaps you'll think of a thing or two.
Then it will all pass, and you'll be pure crystal.
And then love.

Narcissus was so much in love with himself.
Only a fool doesn't see that he loved the river too.   20
You sit alone.
Your heart pains you, but it's not going to break.
The faded dramatis personae are erased one by one.
Then the flaws are erased. Then a sun
sets at midnight. You remember   25
the dark flowers too.
You wish you were dead or alive or anyone else.
Isn't there even one country you love?
Isn't there even one word?
Surely you remember.   30
Only a fool lets the sun set at its own pleasure.
It always sets off too early westward for the islands.
Sun and moon, winter and summer will come to you.
Infinite treasure.

Title, *You*. The addressee is masculine.

The Dress

Two Garden Songs

Giants

Some ants found half a carcass of a fly
and what a time they had
hauling it out of the grass.
Their little hips nearly split with the labor.
And of all things, suddenly the grass   5
swelled and made sheaves like a barley field.
Isn't it crazy for grass to think it's a barley field.
I knew the ants would come to a bitter end—
all that hard work and an early death.
A few husky insects strutted about in the grass,   10
whistling at those foolish ants.
Each flower grew to the best of its ability,
the roses more showy than in years past.
And then I wept.
All of them around me had become such giants.   15

All of Them Growing

A swarm of gnats seethes every day at six.
It's growing hunchback, my pathetic grass.
Each day again there's something I desire.
The sun no longer resembles a ball of fire,
On the inside, the sun is seething.   20

Lines 1–11, *ants.* Calling into question Prov. 6:6–8, "Go to the ant, thou sluggard; consider her ways and be wise"; cf. also Prov. 30:25.

No air to breathe, there is only pleading.
I tell you, if this summer should finally pass,
everything will be restored:
the flower to the plant, the wing to the bird,
the sand that wandered away to the shore.   25
With a few stalks of corn and some aphid-stricken leaves
it's impossible to live.
I tell you it's impossible to live.
So many just grow and grow, and hardly anyone is in bloom.

How Hong Kong Was Destroyed

I am in Hong Kong.
There's a tongue of a river there crawling with snakes.
There are Greeks, Chinese, blacks.
Near the paper lanterns, carnival crocodiles
crack open their jaws.   5
Who said they eat you alive here?
Hordes of people went down to the river.
You've never seen such silk in your life,
redder than poppy blossoms.

In Hong Kong   10
the sun rises in the East
and they water the flowers with a perfumed spray
to redouble their scent.
But when evening comes, a wind lashes the paper lanterns
and if someone's murdered, they ask   15
Was he Chinese? Black?
Did he die in agony?
Then they pitch his body into the river
and all the bottom-feeders gorge.

I am in Hong Kong.   20
In the evening the café lights dim
and scores of paper lanterns rip in the streets.
And the earth seethes and explodes,

seethes and explodes,
and I alone know   25
there is nothing in the West
and nothing in the East.
The paper dragon yawns
but the earth keeps exploding.
Hordes of enemies are headed here   30
who've never seen silk in their lives.

Only the little whores, dressed in soiled silk,
still receive their guests
in tiny alcoves hung with lanterns.
In the morning some of them weep   35
over their rotting flesh.
And if someone's killed, they ask,
Ay ay, Chinese? Black?
Poor thing, let's hope he didn't die in agony.
And already at dusk the first guests arrive   40
like a thorn in the living flesh.
I am in Hong Kong
and Hong Kong is on the ocean,
hanging like a colored lantern on a hook at the edge of the world.
Maybe the dragon   45
will swathe her in crimson silk
and cast her
into the abyss of the stars.
And only the little whores will sob into their silks
for even now   50
still now
men are pinching them in the belly.

I am not in Hong Kong
and Hong Kong is not in the world.
Where there once was a Hong Kong   55
there's a single pink stain
half in the water and half in the sky.

Line 41, *a thorn in the living flesh*. Plays on the rabbinic saying, "The worm is as griev-
ous to the dead as a needle in the living flesh," Tractate *Berakhot* 18:72; cf. 2 Cor.
12:7, "a thorn in the flesh."

The Dress

for Yitzhak Livni

You know, she said, they made you a dress of fire.
Remember how Jason's wife burned in her dress?
It was Medea, she said, Medea did that to her.
You've got to be careful, she said,
they made you a dress that glows like an ember,   5
that burns like coals of fire.

Are you going to wear it, she said, don't wear it.
It's not the wind whistling, it's the poison seething.
You're not even a princess, what can you do to Medea?
Can't you tell one sound from another, she said,   10
it's not the wind whistling.

Remember, I told her, that time when I was six?
They shampooed my hair and I went out into the street.
The scent of shampoo trailed after me like a cloud.
Then the wind and the rain made me ill.   15
I didn't know yet how to read Greek tragedies,
but that fragrance filled the air and I was very ill.
Now I can tell that perfume was unnatural.

What will become of you, she said,
they made you a burning dress.   20
They made me a burning dress, I said. I know.
So why are you standing there, she said, you ought to beware.
Don't you know what that means, a burning dress?

I know, I said, but not to beware.
The scent of that perfume confuses me.   25
I said to her: No one has to agree with me,
I don't put my trust in Greek tragedy.

Dedication, *Yitzhak Livni*. Ravikovitch's second husband and lifelong friend.
Lines 5–6, *ember . . . coals of fire* (Heb. *remetz, gechalim*). See "But She Had a Son."

But the dress, she said, the dress is on fire.
What are you saying, I shouted, what are you saying?
I'm not wearing a dress at all, can't you see
what's burning is me.

The Bullfrogs

for Leah Goldberg

The starry sky is a bottomless sea.
On a night such as this, it's easy to see
how deep the Slough of Despond must be.
In a crowd of bullfrogs, in a little pond,
there's a yellow lily, dwelling apart.
Only the wondrous courage of her heart
keeps her from seeking another pond.
On a night such as this, it's easy to know
what kind of man would rape women,
gagging them with the palm of his hand.

The starry sky is a bottomless sea,
her face fretted with golden furrows.
Where once Prometheus was bound to the rock,
a Greek fisherman stands
these eight long years.
In the moon of Tammuz the breezes revive him
but the cold of winter galls his skin.
Over the course of these eight years
his head has grown bald and bare as the rock.

Dedication, *Leah Goldberg* (1911–1970). The major woman poet of the pre-State Hebrew modernists; Ravikovitch's literary mentor and model for Israeli women poets. This homage is written in Goldberg's style. See "The Captors Require a Song."

Line 4, *bullfrogs* (Heb. *karpodim*, masc.), a neologism, instead of the normative *karpadot* (female frogs) or *tzfarde'im* (male frogs). A fable about the many male poets and the one female poet in the literary pond. *a little pond*. An allusion to Bialik's "The Pond."

Line 16, *moon of Tammuz*. See "Like the Rolling Dust before the Whirlwind."

Now I see his wasted eyes   20
and astounded, I cry out.
The stars are seething in the deep.
Tonight they too will speak their piece.

Like that marvelous yellow water lily,
many won't reach another pond.   25
As for the bullfrogs, they are too blind to fathom
the dread terror of our hearts.

Waning and Waxing

Now the moon's
on the wane,
he parches and wilts,
withers and sets.
And yet   5
perhaps the rainclouds have swelled his belly
as if his waning were done.
A thin veil stretches across the sky.
The moon wanes and sets
as if lopped off,   10
as if about to drop.
These fleecy clouds
have plagued him with blight.
But wait—
behind him   15
a pale disk rises:
The full moon of the half month
that crossed the sky before
now shines once more.
Light as a seed between sky-webs   20

Line 3, *he*. The common Hebrew word for "moon," *yare'ach*, masc., as distinguished from the more poetic *levana*, fem., as in "The Moon in the Rain."

Line 17, *moon of the half month*. In the Jewish (lunar) calendar, the middle of the month coincides with the full moon.

or fat as a ripened gourd.
Now the moon's on the wane,
now the moon drops.
Look at him, love, come look:
He always comes back.   25

In the Right Wind

The End of the Fall

If a man falls from a plane in the middle of the night
God alone can raise him.
God appears at his side in the middle of the night,
touches the man and soothes his agony.
God does not wipe away his blood   5
for the blood is not life,
God does not coddle his body
for the man is not flesh.
God leans over him, lifts up his head and gazes at him.
In God's eyes the man is a little child.   10
He gets up clumsily on all fours and wants to walk,
then senses he has wings to fly.
The man is still confused: He doesn't know
it feels better to hover than to crawl.
God wishes to stroke his head   15
though he tarries;
he would not want to frighten the man
with portents of love.

Line 1, *falls from a plane*. This poem is usually read as alluding to the life and work of Antoine de Saint-Exupéry, author of *The Little Prince*. His plane crash in 1944 while piloting a wartime reconnaissance mission was an unresolved mystery when the poem was written. See "Antoine de Saint-Exupéry, In Memoriam."

Lines 6, 8, *blood . . . life . . . flesh*. Reversing the basis for the law in Deut. 12:23, "for the blood is the life"; cf. Gen. 9:4, Lev. 17:11.

Line 16, *though he tarries*. The Hebrew verb *mitmahameha* is associated with the delayed coming of the Messiah: "though he tarry, yet do I believe." From Maimonides' Thirteen Principles, recited in the morning prayers.

If a man falls from a plane in the middle of the night
God alone knows the end of the fall.   *20*

In the Right Wind

When a man sits alone in a room
what do outsiders know about him?
There may be a humming in his ears
twenty-four hours a day.
And some people just don't see   *5*
how hard it is for him to bear the day.
Morning doesn't shine as it ought to,
the face of the sun is like a crushed disk,
and some people can't even feel
how ugly a crushed disk can be.   *10*

Twenty-five years ago
a terrible war took hold of the world.
Among the thousands of houses that fell
were people whose hearts were full.
The man sitting alone in his room   *15*
keeps gazing at the crushed sun.
He begins to reflect on wondrous things.
Like flying in the right wind.
Some people can fly without even needing
the right wind.   *20*
Pine branches catch at their cheeks,
they fly with moist open lips.
Then a bit of cloud-dust or a floating speck
unwittingly kisses them on the lips.
Their eyes shine, awash in tears   *25*
at the sky's amazing blue.
When some heavenly body brushes against them,
it does them no harm.

Title, *In the Right Wind*. The primary meaning of *ru'ach* is "wind"; it can also mean
"spirit." Cf. Gen. 1:2.

Flying means that the layers of air
bear you up, as in loving.   *30*
You lift off, you land.
And this may surprise you:
Some people fly in the right wind
and are cut down, suddenly, before their time.

The Imagination's a Thing That Hath No Measure

The everlasting jungles won't last forever
if lightning strikes them,
from distant lands come rumors
about tremors of the earth.
I'm no longer taken in by the Vision of the Yellow River   *5*
for the river has nothing in it but water
and even that in the end runs into one of the seas.
The imagination's a thing that hath no measure
but by the laws of pure reason
is the Black Sea any different from the Caspian Sea?   *10*
A person of thirty is not like a child.
He stops hoping for miracles, won't be seduced by a little rustling.
He won't lose his head, not even after sunset
when the marvelous sea darkens and conceals its sharks.
But those rumors keep coming back: *15*
            Rumor is something that can't be restrained.
Rumor drives rumor around the world
as wind drives the waves.
First they bear you up as the river bears Ophelia,
then they sweep you down into the darkest of deep currents   *20*
and all your youthful dreams, all your imagination, won't drag you
out of the waters.

Title, *Hath No Measure*. Rabbinic category for commandments (Heb. *mitzvot*) of which one can never perform too many; for example, the study of Torah (Tractate *Pe'ah* 1:1).

Line 7, *runs into one of the seas.* Eccl. 1:7.

The Horns of Hittin

In the morning strange ships were floating on the sea,
prow and stern in the ancient style.
In the eleventh century
Crusader caravans set sail,
riffraff and kings.   5
Crates of gold and plunder weltered in the ports,
ships of gold
piers of gold.
The sun set marvelous fires in them,
flaming forests.   10
When the sun dazzled and the waves surged,
their hearts went out to Byzantium.
How cruel and naive those Crusaders were.
They plundered everything.

The villagers were gripped by a boundless terror.   15
Their daughters were carried off by force,
their blue-eyed grandsons were sired
in disgrace.
No one spared their honor.

Slender-necked ships set sail for Egypt.   20
As if electrified, the gorgeous troops marched upon Acre.
Swift knights all, bearing the Bishop's blessing.
A great flock of wolves.
How their blue eyes shone
when they saw the palm trees swaying in the wind.   25
How they soiled their beards with spittle
when they dragged women into the thicket.

Title, *Horns of Hittin*. Site of a celebrated hillside battle near the Sea of Galilee, in
which Saladin decisively defeated the Crusader armies in 1187; the hill has two peaks
resembling horns.

Line 5, *riffraff*. A contemptuous term in the Exodus story for the motley throng among
the Israelites who departed from Egypt, Exod. 12:38.

Line 15, *villagers* (Heb. *kafri'yim*). A contemporary term for the rural Palestinian
population.

Many fortresses they built,
snipers' towers, ramparts of basalt.
In the villages their bastards, now full grown,　　　　　　　*30*
marveled at them.

In the twelfth century
the Marquis of Montfort's eye grew dim.
The winds of Galilee hissed over his gloomy fortress.
A curved scimitar burst from the East　　　　　　　　　　*35*
like a jester's staff.
Saladin advanced from the East in motley garb.
With the horns of a wild ox
he gored them hip and thigh, that infidel dog:
Saladin　　　　　　　　　　　　　　　　　　　　　　*40*
did them in
at the Horns of Hittin.

Thenceforth they had no dominion,
no life eternal, no Jerusalem.
How cruel and naive those Crusaders were.　　　　　　　*45*
They plundered everything.

Line 33, *Marquis of Montfort*. Conrad de Montferrat, one of the Crusader rulers of
Palestine. *grew dim* (Heb. *kahata eyno*). Unlike Moses's vigor and vision in advanced
old age, Deut. 34:7.

Line 34, *his gloomy fortress*. The stronghold of Montfort, built to protect Acre (Akko),
a coastal city in the Western Galilee; the ruins of the fortress still stand today.

Line 38, *horns of a wild ox*. Deut. 33:17, "His horns are the horns of a wild ox; with
them he gores the peoples" (NRSV).

Line 39, *hip and thigh*. Judges 15:8, Samson's defeat of the Philistines.

The Viking

Portrait

She sits in the house for days on end.
She reads the paper.
(Come on, don't you?)
She doesn't do what she'd like to do,
she's got inhibitions.   5
She wants vanilla, lots of vanilla,
give her vanilla.

In winter she's cold, really cold,
colder than other people.
She bundles up but she's still cold.   10
She wants vanilla.

She wasn't born yesterday, if that's what you're thinking.
It's not the first time she's cold.
Not the first time it's winter.
In fact summer isn't so pleasant either.   15
She reads the paper more than she'd like to.

In winter she won't budge without the heater.
Sometimes she gets fed up with it all.
Has she ever asked that much of you?
Admit it: She hasn't.   20
She wants vanilla.

*   *   *

Line 7, *give her vanilla*. The addressee of the speaker's command in Hebrew is in the masculine singular.

Should you care to look closer, she's wearing a plaid skirt.
She likes a plaid skirt because it's cheery.
Just to look at her, you'd laugh.
It's all so ludicrous. 25
Even she laughs about it on occasion.
She has a hard time in winter,
a rough time in summer,
you'd laugh.
One might say mimosa, 30
a bird that won't fly,
there's plenty of things one might say.
She's always bundling up in something or other
until she chokes,
on occasion a plaid skirt and other clothes. 35
Why bundle up if it makes her choke, you'd ask.
These things are complicated.

It's the cold in winter, the exaggerated heat in summer,
never what you need.
And by the way, don't you forget, she wants vanilla. 40
Now she's even crying.
Give her vanilla.

Two Ships Burning

Two tankers burning in the Atlantic
off the coast of Spain.
Announced on the radio.
Other ships rush to the rescue
in search of survivors. 5
Whoever gets out of a fire alive
will usually bow down low
kiss the ground
believe in God.
On the face of it, what a strange thing: to burn in water. 10

Lines 6–9, *Whoever . . . believe in God.* Cf. 2 Chron. 7:3, "they bowed themselves
with their faces to the ground . . . and praised the Lord."

When you get down to it, there's nothing more terrible.
One must take into account
that not everyone will survive.
Meanwhile the rescue teams are racing
into the water.   15
People just love to rescue something from the waves.

Now the sun gutters out in the water.
A fire won't stop for the night,
won't stop of its own accord
till they extinguish it.   20
I do hope everyone gets out alive.
How cruel the memories that are wakened
by the four million dead of Franco's war.

Australia

1

Down south in the world—Australia,
island of summer rain,
less than one inhabitant
per square kilometer.
What do the settlers of Australia   5
do with those cold June nights,
that warm Christmas,
the monsoon rains?
Down south in the world—Australia,
a continent without a people,   10
farther away than Malaysia,
farther than Singapore.
On the map, Australia
floats along in the ocean
as if it weren't far at all   15
from the South Pole.

*   *   *

Line 23, *Franco's war*. Opposing Franco during the Spanish Civil War (1936–1939)
was a sacred cause in Socialist Zionism.

How idyllic, you might say:
sheepshearing in Australia.
Gold diggers made their way to her,
those white settlers.   20
They wasted their days for nought,
all alone.
No women, none.

How far away, Australia.
Only the kangaroo hops around there—   25
that human animal
who carries her young on her belly.

        2
Down south in the garden,
where the sprinkler doesn't reach,
it's like Australia.   30
Arid. Stunted shrubbery,
swarms of nomadic ants,
wild bees.
The ground is dry
and the lawn has a hard time growing.   35
Only wild grasses spread there, as in the jungle.
Like wild men dancing around the fire.

A Private Opinion

Pain is a useless thing,
I can tell you,
the way a worm crawling inside a piece of fruit
won't make it taste any better.
I know you,   5
I can see what your youth meant to you
and how twisted your face is getting these days.
No heroes are ever begotten that way.

*   *   *

Heroes are something else again,
I assure you.   10
They're nonvegetal beings.
They fight in the air in the sea even in Manchuria,
always some strange and faraway place.
My heart goes out to them to the air to the sea even to Manchuria—
but let medals and badges not be their motive.   15
As a rule they're used for stoking up locomotives
as in Manchuria,
and I'm sorry to say they die like dogs.

Pain is an inhuman thing,
I would argue,   20
for me there are no extenuating circumstances.
Look, isn't it ugliness incarnate:
someone secretly lost,
blackening away
withering away   25
without a wife, without sons.

Antoine de Saint-Exupéry, In Memoriam

A terrible glowing moon
reminded me in the middle of the night
how in the year nineteen forty-three
Antoine
de Saint-Exupéry died.   5

It's been twenty-one years now
and bits of paper are whirling in the wind.
For twenty-one years
the sea keeps turning blue each spring,

Title, *Antoine de Saint-Exupéry*. French writer and aviator, author of *The Little Prince*.

Line 3, *nineteen forty-three*. Saint-Exupéry in fact crashed while flying a secret mission for the Allies on July 31, 1944; he had survived several earlier crashes. See "The End of the Fall."

twenty-one years   *10*
and all his bones decomposed into sand.
Twenty-one,
twenty-one,
and whoever's alive now is alive without him.
Twenty-one years ago   *15*
his plane plunged into the Mediterranean
teetering between the rough winds of spring.

It's not the same world anymore,
grass and wind,
wind and sand.   *20*
That's the look of a world
in which there is no
Saint-Exupéry.

People don't live forever,
even we won't forever,   *25*
but if he'd been rescued
that time
in March, in the year nineteen forty-three,
he'd be with us still
a glowing speck,   *30*
lily in the wind,
laughter in the clouds.

The Viking

for Richard Swanson of Chicago

With Richard
everything was twisted: the face, the arms.
A crazy eleven-year-old kid.
In the garden behind the museum,
after a pitiful lunch,   *5*

Epigraph, *Richard Swanson of Chicago*. According to Ravikovitch, Swanson was a resi-
dent at the Orthogenic School at the University of Chicago, a facility for emotionally
disturbed children. Ravikovitch worked there under Bruno Bettelheim's direction.

he talked to the squirrels
at the top of his lungs,
and it goes without saying
the squirrels ran for their lives.
"I wasn't trying to hurt them, really I wasn't,"   10
said Richard later,
"just to give them a scare."
Richard
always dirty, his head somewhere else.
There on the shore of the lake   15
I was afraid he'd disappeared again.
Then I saw him swimming and messing around,
in the freezing muddy water
he was having the time of his life.
There isn't a single bad thing   20
that can't be said about Richard,
they even said he's bursting with envy.
Nonetheless, it should be noted
that Richard was a Viking,
tall and slender, unsullied behind his mask.   25
In the murky muddy water,
in the museum grove
when he made himself the laughingstock
of the squirrels and the assembled crowd,
his marvelous eyes   30
were fixed on the distance in a crazy gaze.
Richard dreamt of setting the world to rights
more than anyone else I know.

I could always imagine
those ancient forefathers of his   35
sailing like madmen
in an odd-looking ship across the North Sea.
How they cut through the snows,
comic in their lanky bearing.
How they perished in astonishment,   40
having grown rather intimate
with misery and frost,
and yet in innocence,
without sufficient knowledge.

    *   *   *

Richard,   45
crazy kid.
Even great gardeners
who have hothouses filled with orchids and exotic plants,
who have in their ponds
white swans and black,   50
will never be able to grow
anything so beautiful as Richard,
my love.

In Chad and Cameroon

By the oases of Chad and Cameroon
European settlers sit around all afternoon,
despairing of life.
They no longer care about manners.
Not far from them a band of lepers   5
passes by.
The elders with no fingers.
At eventide, no wind in the sky.
It's as hot as always. But then
a pinkish glow rises from the waters   10
in Chad and Cameroon
and falls upon the European men.

Pride

Even rocks crack, I tell you,
and not on account of age.
For years they lie on their backs in the cold and the heat,
so many years,
it almost creates the impression of calm.   5
They don't move, so the cracks can hide.

Title, *Chad and Cameroon*. Former colonies of France and Britain.

A kind of pride.
Years pass over them as they wait.
Whoever is going to shatter them
hasn't come yet.   10
And so the moss flourishes, the seaweed is cast about,
the sea bursts out and slides back,
and it seems the rocks are perfectly still.
Till a little seal comes to rub against them,
comes and goes.   15
And suddenly the stone has an open wound.
I told you, when rocks crack, it happens by surprise.
Not to mention people.

Line 12, *bursts out*. Judges 20:33, of enemies in ambush (REB).

The Marionette

Even for a Thousand Years

I cannot bring a world quite round
and there's no sense trying.
Day unto day and day unto night utter nothing.
Sweet peas, margosas and roses bloom in the spring,
all of them life size and in full color.   5
The truly original doesn't sprout up here,
not once in ten years.
Whoever wants to breathe attar of roses
let him gather it from the wind,
and whoever wants to plant a tree   10
let him plant a fig tree
for the benefit of generations to come.

Ask me if I've ever seen beauty
and I'll answer, Yes, quite a bit,
but not where it should be.   15
Say, that cataract on the river:
Of course I've seen it,
so what?
Mighty waterfalls are not such a pleasant sight.
The truly beautiful doesn't stroll around outside,   20
sometimes it comes to pass in a room

Line 3, *Day unto day*. Reversing Psalm 19:2, "Day unto day uttereth speech, and night unto night showeth knowledge."

Line 4, *margosas* (Heb. *izdarekhet*). Ornamental Israeli trees, whose fruit is poisonous.

when the doors are locked, the shutters drawn tight.
The truth is, a thing of beauty
isn't a river or a mountain or an ocean view.
I know too much about all of them to delude myself   25
and think up something new.

What's left after the pain is just curiosity
to see how things turn out,
what they'll come to in the end,
all those beautiful things.   30

I know: I don't have to plant a fig tree.
There are other options.
One could always wait for spring, roses and gladioli.
But time makes people grow tough as fingernails,
gray as rocks   35
stubborn as stone.
It's a seductive prospect, perhaps—to turn into a block of salt.
With a mineral power.
To stare empty-eyed at this potash and phosphate factory
even for a thousand years.   40

Next Year

for Gila Dror

What are you sitting here for,
you've got no other place?
What is she sitting here for,
like some kind of lizard?
She's got no place.   5
Yesterday you saw something better.
Or maybe last year.
Get out of this Vale of Tears.

＊   ＊   ＊

Line 39, *potash and phosphate factory*. The Dead Sea Works near Sodom.

Line 8, *Vale of Tears* (Heb. *emek ha-bakha*). Literal translation of Psalm 84:6. Cf.
Vulgate.

All that withering in the leaves,
all that dust,   *10*
those sheets of paper that I tore.
I don't want to see it anymore.
I have no patience.

And yesterday a see-through nymph arose from the sea
all green and blue.   *15*
Only a boor would call her Medusa.
I've got my flaws too.
But not of that kind.

This place is out of the question now.
So much insult and so much dust.   *20*
If you have no use for these people,
leave them.

The wind delivers dust, and you can't shake off people, either.
Sometimes I think that like rats they deliver the plague,
God only help them,   *25*
and help me too.
There's not an iota of gentleness in them.
And in all the tumult, they listen to the news:
Once again Abba Eban
has delivered an historic address.   *30*

What are you sitting here for, always at a loss,
always scared of what's going to be?
Just give it a try, for once,
remember what it says in the books—
get out of this Vale of Tears.   *35*

Next year
in Jerusalem.

Line 16, *Medusa* (Heb. *meduza*). Also the word for "jellyfish."

Line 29, *Abba Eban* (1915–2002). Israeli diplomat and statesman, known for his ornate rhetorical style.

Lines 36–37, *Next year in Jerusalem*. Recited by Jews in the Diaspora at the end of the Passover Seder. Ravikovitch chooses this version instead of the one recited in Israel: "Next year in the rebuilt Jerusalem."

What's Happening

Reuven Malka
got hold of an assault rifle.
What's happening to us?
At the first rain they handed out medals of honor
to the incredible untrainable dead.   5
At the first rain, another army patrol
stepped on a Czech-made mine
and guerillas trained in North Vietnam
hid out in the thicket.
What's happening to us?   10
Tales of heroism that rack up the medals
wreck our imagination.
What's happening?
Men who fell last spring
now seem a thousand years old.   15
In the desert close to Rafah,
a palm tree grew.
Strange but true.
From the legendary body of Avshalom Feinberg.
Strange but true: 20
A state funeral awaits him.
A purple heart too.
A handshake, courtesy of the Commander in Chief.
And today the wind growls on the Golan Heights
like a rabid bitch.   25
What's happening to us?

In a landslide of color the world is a-whirling,
the times are a-changing,

Line 9, *thicket* (Heb. *svakh*). Gen. 22:13, "a ram caught in a thicket by his horns."

Line 19, *Avshalom Feinberg* (1889–1917). One of the leaders of NILI, an underground movement during World War I, who was murdered near Rafah; according to legend, a palm tree sprang from his grave. His remains were reinterred on Mount Herzl with full military honors in 1967.

Line 24, *Golan Heights.* Syrian territory occupied and annexed by Israel in 1967.

and off he goes to guard duty again, Private Malka
with his standard-issue rifle and two hand grenades.   *30*
Long may he live, Private Malka!
No more purple hearts.
No more heroic tales.
Let them get a little satisfaction,
Private Malka and his seven brothers.   *35*

A Pure Whole Memory

Only when the face is erased
can anything here be remembered whole,
only when the face is erased.
Then the lights go wild,
the colors start from their frames.   *5*
Stars plunge from their height like epileptics.
Grasses groan up out of the earth
(their growing pains greater than withering-pangs).

All those things that blind our eyes
draw back to the shadows.   *10*
So too the face.
Something stirs in the depths.

How many days
how many years, wind and weather,
have we waited for it to erupt   *15*
from the depths of the earth,
one pure whole memory
like a lily,
pale red.

The Marionette

To be a marionette.
In this precious gray predawn light
to sweep under the new day,
diving down
through the undercurrents.   5
To be a marionette,
a pale slender doll of porcelain
hanging by a thread.

To be a marionette.
And the threads that wreathe my life   10
are genuine silk.
A marionette
also has her reality.
She has her memories.

Four hundred years ago   15
there was a Donna Elvira, Contessa of Seville,
with her three hundred maidservants.
But only when she beheld
that handkerchief of fine silk
did she know her end: 20
to be a porcelain marionette
or a waxen doll.

Donna Elvira, Contessa of Seville, dreamt of late-ripening vines.
Her knights always spoke to her in dulcet tones.
Donna Elvira, Contessa et cetera, was gathered unto her people.   25
She left two sons and a daughter
to a gloomy future.
In the twentieth century, on a precious gray dawn,

Line 10, *wreathe* (Heb. *suga*). Cf. Song of Songs 7:3.

Line 16, *Donna Elvira*. Seduced and betrayed by Don Giovanni in the Mozart opera.

how fortunate to be a marionette.
This woman is not responsible for her actions,   30
the judges opine.
Her fragile heart is gray as the dawn,
her body hangs by a thread.

DEEP

CALLETH

Day unto Day Uttereth Speech

As in the forests of Carmel
where my soul went out in yearning
with the wind of day,
the pines dropped their needles,
pinecones kept falling to the ground.   5
My house was sealed with drapes
I sewed of Cathay silk
but light kept piercing the portals,
light kept flooding the sills.

There we passed our lives   10
unawares,
I never set eyes on the Book of Days.
King David joined me
after he rose to return from the dead.
Day after day he would sit by my side,   15
when his heart was glad
he would play hymns of praise:
The heavens declare the glory of God.

As in the forests of Carmel
pinecones without measure kept falling, falling.   20

King over Israel

for Yitzhak Livni

Always in the backseat of the car,
the face of heaven arid as a field of thorns.
My eyes could find no resting place
from one end of heaven to the other.

Title, *Day unto Day Uttereth Speech*. Psalm 19:2. See "Even for a Thousand Years."

Line 2, *my soul . . . yearning.* Psalm 84:2, lit. "my soul goes out in yearning for the courts of the Lord."

White nights 5
are ghastly as the face of a beast
baring its teeth at a desert bush.
But nights black as chimney soot
were no better in my eyes.

This Dead Sea has no water for the thirsty, 10
no resting place for my eyes in the coursing of the stars.
So many years in the backseat
like a field passed over by the rain.

This field has no water for the thirsty.

The man who walked the streets of Jerusalem, 15
a crown of thorns on his head to mock him,
he is the man who knew the meaning of a field
with no sign of water for the thirsty.

The man who ascended the streets of Jerusalem,
and from the beginning saw his end before him, 20
torments weighed upon his heart
when he saw that even the heavens
were arid as a field of thorns.

And I, in the backseat,
so many years in the backseat, 25
I too knew not to put my trust
in ships that appear to be sailing on the sea.

I, Koheleth, was king over Israel in Jerusalem.

How the city sat solitary.

Line 28, *Koheleth*. The name of the speaker in the Book of Ecclesiastes; from the Hebrew root *kahal*, "congregation, assembly," translated in Eccl. 1:12 as "the Preacher."

Line 29, *How the city sat solitary*. The opening words of the Book of Lamentations about the destruction of Jerusalem: "How doth the city sit solitary, that was full of people; how is she become a widow!"

Midnight Song 1970

Once again, as in years past,
the bedroom's a mess,
cigarette ashes knee deep,
clothes dropped in a heap,
a pile of mail that I haven't read   5
and one warm bed.
There's a flu epidemic going around
and here I am, good and sick,
flat on my back.
This year   10
and in all the years to come,
I won't give up one tiny bird
that flutters about in my garden,
won't trade one tiny bird
for a hoopoe or a dove.   15
Another year will come
and once again, without fail,
my throat will be choking with love.

This Nightmare

Why is it always the same nightmare?
Trains streak by like the deer of the field
but none will ever arrive anywhere.
On the map there is no Land of Israel;
perhaps there wasn't yet a Land of Israel.   5
Herzl is brewing up schemes in his heart

Line 15, *hoopoe, dove*. Symbolic birds prominent in Jewish folklore and literature.

Line 4, *Land of Israel* (Heb. *Eretz Yisra'el*). Pre-state Palestine; also the nationalist term for the Greater Israel, including the post-1967 Occupied Territories.

Line 6, *Herzl*. Theodor Herzl (1860–1904), founder of modern political Zionism.

but Weizmann is always the shrewder one.
A Zionist Congress meets here yet again
and a little child doth lead them all.
Why is it always the same nightmare?   10

The grasses of yesteryear are no more
and Jerusalem too has slipped out of bounds.
Trains keep running but never arrive
and over the grasses a ghastly mist.
Weizmann's beard tangles with Herzl's beard   15
and the people cry out for Ben-Gurion,
even the handful of famished old folk
who came here and couldn't find their ground.
Why is it always the same nightmare?

It always comes back, the same nightmare.   20
Just this Thursday a soldier was killed.
Shammai Cohen, clever boy,
grew like a palm tree, grew and is gone.
Shammai Cohen, killed at the Canal,
and the whole house of Israel will weep for him.   25
No stranger dare take a seat where he sat
and over the mountains a ghastly mist.
When I return to Jerusalem again
I shall ask how he fares, Shammai Cohen.
There shall a mist burst forth from the sun   30
and the Zionist Congress shall be no more.

*   *   *

Line 7, *Weizmann*. Chaim Weizmann (1874–1952), first President of the State of
Israel.

Line 8, *Zionist Congress*. Held in Europe between 1897 and 1946, and in Jerusalem
since statehood.

Line 9, *a little child doth lead them*. An ironic allusion to Isa. 11:6, a vision of peace
on earth, invoked nonironically in line 37.

Line 16, *Ben-Gurion*. David Ben-Gurion (1886–1973), first Prime Minister of Israel.
Served in that capacity in 1948–1953 and 1955–1963; retired from politics in 1970,
but remained the icon of a strong leader.

Line 23, *like a palm tree*. Psalm 92:12.

Line 24, *Canal*. The Suez Canal, site of the War of Attrition between Israel and Egypt,
1968–1970.

And over Ein Karem, steeped in that light,
I'll weep at last for Shammai Cohen
who shone out like Jerusalem's light
and one day was brought to eternal rest.   35
And then shall the land slip from its mooring
and a little child shall lead them all.

All Thy Breakers and Waves

And I beheld the tear of the oppressed
turning to naught on their cheeks.
The scent of wild daisies rose from the ravines
and a sprightly scent of acacia.
And the waters of the brook   5
crashed upon the rocks
in a wave of vain mirth.
At the Sea of Galilee there were bathers on the banks
but no wind stirred.
There was no one to walk upon the water,   10
just a bunch of boats and water sports.
And I beheld the tear of the oppressed.

Whoever wants to partake of the light,
it's his to possess.
And every man shall be free as a crane   15
to come and go as he please,
except for one
who is mine.
How good it is for the eyes to behold the light
and the waters so sweet and blessed   20

Line 32, *Ein Karem*. A neighborhood in the hills of Jerusalem.

Title, *All Thy Breakers and Waves*. Psalm 42:7, cf. Jonah 2:3. See "Deep unto Deep."

Line 1, *tear of the oppressed*. Eccl. 4:1, "Behold, the tears [Heb. singular] of such as were oppressed, and they had no comforter."

and the tear of the oppressed
so bitter.

Growing Poor

If I am to grow poor
let it be like a land
ravaged by blight.
If I am to grow poor
let it be with pride.   5
Torah scrolls
are saved from the fire.
Not me.
If I die, this is my desire:
Let me be   10
like some ship wrecked at sea.
Waters without end
will extinguish the fire.

Negligible Sand

That time too we walked back to the beach again
and again I said but how will it end
and he said it's too soon to talk,
too bad, but subject to change.
And again I said time after time   5
and time after time
he keeps telling me that, or he tries
to talk about anything but.

 * * *

Line 11, *ship wrecked at sea.* See "Two Ships Burning" and "Many Waters."

Lines 12–13, *Waters . . . fire.* Reversing Song of Songs 8:7, lit. "Many waters will not extinguish the fire of love."

And again we embraced for an hour or so
and even went looking for a more scenic spot. 10
When it got late we shook out our clothes
and again I hinted that shouldn't we consider,
and again I said it's like crumbling sand,
and what he answered slips my mind.
And there, in fact, 15
there by the sea,
everything slipped through my fingers like sand.

From Day to Night

Every day I rise from sleep again
as if for the last time.
I don't know what awaits me,
perhaps it follows logically, then,
that nothing awaits me. 5
The spring on its way
is like the spring gone by.
I know about the month of May
but pay it no mind.
For me there's no border between night and day, 10
just that night is colder
though silence is equal to them both.
At dawn I hear the voices of birds.
I fall asleep easily
out of affection for them. 15
The one who is dear to me is not here,
perhaps he simply is not.
I cross over from day to night
from day to day
like a feather 20
the bird doesn't feel as it falls away.

The Sound of Birds at Noon

This chirping
is surely not vicious.
They sing without giving us a thought
and they are as numerous
as the seed of Abraham.   5
They have a life of their own,
flight for them is no act of the mind.
Some are prized, others despised,
but the wing itself is beauty.
Their hearts aren't heavy   10
even when they peck at a worm.
Perhaps they're light-minded.
The heavens were given to them
for dominion over day and night
and the moment they alight on a branch,   15
the branch too is theirs.
This chirping is entirely free of malice.
Over the years it may even
appear
to carry a note of compassion.   20

Hide and Seek

Some things I forget,
others I retain.
My childhood glided away
and I remain.
The honeysucker too   5
glides from branch to branch
from mote to beam
and I look on.
There's something or other behind the wall

Line 7, *mote to beam*. Tractate *Nezikin* 15; cf. Matt. 7:3.

or the door: *10*
a memory that uproots mountains
and grinds one upon the other.
Once I loved an Italian
statue.

When I'm in love I'm condensed as a cloud   *15*
laden with rain,
shedding torrents.
When I'm in love
I'm anything
that may come to a man's mind.   *20*

I ask
with a quizzical look:
What else can happen to me
that hasn't happened to me yet?
I dangle from a cloud   *25*
without wings, without a beak
but I don't fall.
Once when I was in love
I could no longer feel
the cold or the heat.   *30*

Who Art Thou, O Great Mountain

Afternoon light
in Jerusalem,
on the walls above Mamilla Park,

Lines 11–12, *uproots mountains . . . the other*. Talmudic reference to the intellectual prowess of a great scholar; Tractate *Sanhedrin* 24, *Arakhin* 16.

Line 26, *without wings, without a beak*. See "Child Boy Man."

Title, *Who Art Thou, O Great Mountain*. Zech. 4:6–7, "Not by might, nor by power, but by my Spirit, saith the Lord of hosts. Who art thou, O great mountain?"

Line 3, *Mamilla*. An old Jewish-Arab neighborhood in Jerusalem near the 1948 border between Israel and Jordan.

the far reaches of Shlomzion Street
and a cinema dim as a stable.   5
At high noon the sun grew dark for me
that winter.
In the King David Hotel, in the south wing,
in a shop, I would sit
studying Hebrew Lit.   10
Later in Terra Santa
I counted windows above the Pool of Mamilla
and in Talmud class
and Hebrew Grammar
the pupils of my eyes grew wide.   15
I'd nap at noon
and return to Terra Santa,
fourth floor,
mouth agape like a fish.
I was twenty,   20
dazzled, spellbound
by the windows above Mamilla
and the French Hospital,
just before no-man's-land.

I don't need Jerusalem to make me feel grand,   25
not since the sun lost its vigor
and the thistles multiplied.

And Gethsemane I espied
from afar,
and the bus ascending from the church,   30
like some fata morgana above Yemin Moshe.
What good is that to me
now that all the roads are free
and all the dust's grown hard?

Line 11, *Terra Santa*. A number of departments of the Hebrew University held classes
in this building in West Jerusalem after the Mount Scopus campus became inacces-
sible in the 1948 war.

Line 24, *no-man's-land* (Heb. *shetach hefker*). Demilitarized zone separating Israeli
West Jerusalem and Jordanian East Jerusalem, 1948–1967.

Line 31, *Yemin Moshe*. An old quarter of Jerusalem on the 1948 border between Jordan
and Israel near the wall of the Old City.

Deep unto Deep

In Jerusalem I had my days of roses.
What is Jerusalem if not one neighborhood after another?
I came to her young and came back years later
like some odd creature.
Alone   5
in a house not my own,
I lifted mine eyes unto the hills
to see if help was nigh.

There before my eyes
clouds reached out to one another,   10
dark cypresses rustled beneath me.
Suddenly from the ends of the West
an eccentric shard of sun
swooped from on high.

And my longings flooded me like the sea,   15
sawed in my head like a cricket,
swarmed like a hornets' nest—
so delirious was I.

In Jerusalem

At the funeral, of all things.
(The sun was cruel even in winter.)
And I saw Ein Karem,
the monastery and the gardens,
hill upon hill   5
hill under hill.

Title, *Deep unto Deep*. Quoting the opening words of Psalm 42:7, "Deep calleth unto deep at the voice of Your cataracts" (Soncino Bible).

Line 1, *days of roses*, line 18, *delirious*. Cf. the 1962 film, *Days of Wine and Roses*.

Line 7, *I lifted mine eyes unto the hills*. Psalm 121:1.

And here and there in the brush
a monastery roof.

I know where he lives
but not where he's to be found. *10*
For the most part he's not to be found
like a cloud that conceals Jerusalem.

I want to be with him
in the light or in the dark and in Jerusalem too.
Need I say he's beautiful? *15*
How easily I sing his praises.
At the funeral, of all things,
as it moved from Ein Karem to the Mount of Eternal Rest
with so many cars
so many mourners, *20*
I felt a pang of pleasure.
I still wanted to live
perhaps in Jerusalem.
But again I exaggerate.
I wanted him. *25*

Afternoon in Trafalgar Square

Three guys called to me with a wink of the eye
to join them for fun and games
—a Turk and two Spaniards from over the gallery rail
while two fountains were scattering water into the pools.
The smacking drops of water *5*
were cheery as a parrot's sneeze.
The houses, heavy pawed, were daubed thick with soot
but the air was perfectly pure.
I looked a little shopworn, black stockings,

Line 18, *Mount of Eternal Rest* (Heb. *Har Ha-Menuchot*). The major Jewish cemetery
in Jerusalem.

Line 21, *pang of pleasure*. Quoting verbatim Psalm 16:6. The Hebrew *chavalim naflu li
ba-ne'imim* can mean either "My lot . . ." or "My pangs befell me in pleasure."

hair mussed, in my warm plaid dress,   10
hoping in the very worst way for the best,
hoping to make it
even as far as the foot of the Admiral's statue.

Attributes of the Human

Nothing human is alien to me
but it's not especially close to me either.
It's all just a cycle of perpetual return:
One day we
cease to be.   5
The sun stood still on Gibeon
and the moon in the height of sky.
David the son of Jesse, killed Goliath
while still a lad,
but David's grown old and heavy with years   10
and soon the rumor will pass through the marketplace:
The angels above have vanquished the great cliffs below.
Spare the King's honor,
tell it not in Gath.

Like Saul on Gilboa will he be when he dies;   15
no Psalms of Ascents will resound where he lies.

Lines 6–7, *sun . . . moon.* Joshua 10:12–13, "Sun, stand thou still upon Gibeon; and
thou, Moon, in the valley of Ajalon," about Joshua's stalling the natural cycle to achieve
military victory.

Line 12, *The angels above* (Heb. *nitzchu erelim et ha-metzukim,* lit. "the angels above
have overcome the great ones below"). Cf. Midrash *Ecclesiastes Rabbah* 7:18. Said
when a great rabbi dies.

Line 14, *tell it not in Gath.* 2 Sam. 1:20, from King David's lament for Saul and
Jonathan; in modern Hebrew, an ironic idiom about forestalling hostile gossip. See
"Sargeant Major Eyal Sameach."

Line 15, *Like Saul on Gilboa.* Where the wounded king fell on his sword after he was
defeated in battle (1 Sam. 31:1–6).

Line 16, *Psalms of Ascents* (Heb. *shirey ma'alot*). Psalms 120–134, assumed by scholars
to have been sung by pilgrims "ascending" to Jerusalem. The Book of Psalms is tradi-
tionally attributed to David.

But I have no use for any of that.
I'm prepared to shut my eyes and keep still,
seal my lips and keep still.

Like Rachel

To die like Rachel
when the soul shudders like a bird,
wants to break free.
Behind the tent, in fear and dread,
Jacob and Joseph speak of her,   5
a-tremble.
All the days of her life
turn head over heels inside her
like a baby that wants to be born.

How grueling. How   10
Jacob's love ate away at her
with a greedy mouth.
As the soul takes leave now,
she has no use for any of that.

Suddenly the baby screeches,   15
Jacob comes into the tent—
but Rachel does not even sense it.
Rapture washes over her face,
her head.

    *   *   *

Line 1, *like Rachel*. Who died in childbirth, Gen. 35:16–19. Ravikovitch invokes here poems about the biblical Rachel by precursor poets Rachel Marpurgo (1790–1871) and Rachel [Bluvstein] (1890–1931). See "Rough Draft"; cf. "But She Had a Son" and "Lullaby."

Lines 6–7, *speak . . . a-tremble* (Heb. *daber . . . retet*, a hapax), Hos. 13:1.

Line 12, *with a greedy mouth*. Isa. 9:12, a prophecy of how the enemy will devour the Israelites.

Then did a great repose descend upon her.   20
The breath of her nostrils would not stir a feather.
They laid her down among mountain stones
and made her no lament.
To die like Rachel,
that's what I want.   25

Of Wonders beyond My Understanding

Humans who dwell in darkness and the shadow of death,
imprisoned in poverty and iron.

Perhaps in the dullness of my eye
I fail to see the difference
between an eagle in the sky   5
and a scapegoat in the wilderness.

My thoughts keep getting tangled back in themselves.
How easy it is
to go awry.
What I mean to say is: 10
Even a wing is no certainty.

Humans who dwell in darkness and the shadow of death,
imprisoned in poverty and iron—
if their souls be vexed unto death,
then shall their voices ring out   15
and shatter stone.

Title, *Of Wonders Beyond My Understanding*. This poem calls into question Prov. 30:19, which names four wonders of the natural world, including the eagle in line 5.

Lines 1–2, *in darkness . . . and iron*. Psalm 107:10.

Line 6, *scapegoat* (Heb. *sa'ir la-azazel*). Referring to a biblical atonement ritual in which the sins of the community were symbolically laid upon the head of a goat that would then be driven into the wilderness (Lev. 16:10, 21–22).

Line 16, *shatter stone* (Heb. *yeshaber sla'im*). A traditional example of God's power.

Poem of Explanations

Some people know how to love,
for others it's just not right.
Some people kiss in the street
while others would rather not
—and not just in the street.   5
I think it's a talent like any other,
that may be its power.
Like the rose of Sharon
that knows how to flower,
like the lily of the valley   10
that chooses its color.
You know
a rose or a lily in bloom
can dazzle a man's eyes.
I don't mean to offend: 15
I'm aware there's more than one kind.
Honeysuckers are the loveliest of birds
to my mind,
but if someone is so inclined,
let him go to the sparrow.   20
Even so, I keep telling myself,
a sparrow that struts and frets,
a ram with three heads,
an apple that never grows red
—no, that's not me.   25

Line 20, *go to the sparrow*. Echoing Prov. 6:6, "Go to the ant, thou sluggard; consider her ways, and be wise."

Line 22, *a sparrow that struts and frets*. Prov. 30:31 (Heb. *zarzir motnayim*, lit. "sparrow of loins," a hapax). Unclear what animal is designated; the NRSV has "strutting rooster."

Line 23, *ram with three heads* (Heb. *ayil meshulash*, lit. "triple ram," Gen. 15:9). Obscure; usually translated "three-year-old ram." Ravikovitch noted in a letter that she read this as "three-headed."

TRUE

LOVE

for Haim

The Beginning of Silence

I am waiting for the silence,
waiting for the silence to come.
It's beginning to swarm in the corners.
Now it's about to pounce
like a whirlwind.   5
Now it's already touching the red scarf,
now it's touching the far corner of the table,
it cometh nigh.
Tissues in a rainbow box,
the odd-colored chairs   10
here and there around the table.

Now the silence descends like a mighty hand
enfolding the room in a bolt of linen,
enfolding the sea
enfolding the land.   15
The red scarf is the beginning of all things,
beside it—the green chair,
a towel draped over it.

And the silence shrieks inside me
and I shriek inside it.   20
And I look, and behold:
opening, revolving,
entire worlds within the room,
within the wide beam of light
cast by the lamp.   25
And I am quiet and I am calm.

Line 5, *whirlwind*, lines 13–15, *enfolding*. Ezekiel's Chariot Vision (1:4 ff.): "And I looked, and, behold, a whirlwind came out of the north, a great cloud, and a fire enfolding itself. . . ."

Line 12, *like a . . . hand*. Ezek. 1:3, "and the hand of the Lord was there upon him."

Line 22, *revolving*. Cf. the wheels in Ezekiel's Chariot Vision, 1:15–21.

The Finish Line

No,
it's still not
the finish line.
He's missing a few requisite words,
has lost the connections.   5
A lack of clarity,
that's always been his difficulty,
a lack of clarity.

He lifts his eyes to the window:
Shining clouds,   10
the epitome of pure white,
sail across from him
in a distilled azure.

For him, that's a real blow.
He gets restless.   15
For good reason
he finds fault with himself.
He cannot achieve the requisite clarity.

A single feather
flutters above him in the sky,   20
floats slowly by,
hovers again in the wind
with exquisite precision.
Hurrying is not in its repertoire.
At the supper table, the man   25
will seek consolation
in a sprightly yogurt with a spoonful of jam.

　　*　　*　　*

Title and line 32, *The Finish Line* (Heb. *ha-kav ha-acharon*, lit. "the last line"). Raviko-vitch explained the title as referring to "a photo finish, the moment of crossing the finish line in a race."

Line 22, *hovers . . . in the wind*. Cf. Gen. 1:2, lit. "The spirit" or "The wind [Heb. *ru'ach*] of God hovered upon the face of the waters."

No,
he has no reason to respect himself.
Better just peruse the newspaper. Fine.   30
Today won't be the day he'll arrive
at the finish line.

He Will Surely Come

Years tick by me here in a stupor,
absent minded
false minded,
until that tiny head breaks through and dawns,
red as the orb of the setting sun.   5
It will surely come.
The length and breadth of the desert,
hundreds of kilometers round about,
its like is nowhere to be found.
I have tireless powers of forbearance,   10
I sleep late
I wait and wait.
When he comes, he'll be one to behold.
Sometimes I play dead.
When a person comports herself strangely   15
the neighbors cast a critical eye,
whisper behind her back.
With tireless expectation
I breathe upon these slain that they may live.
Only a few dared and lived for a fleeting instant.   20
To the others I was no longer of any use.
I hold my tongue and stop my ears

Title, *He Will Surely Come*. An expression of Jewish messianic yearning, based on
Hab. 2:3, "Though it tarry, wait for it, because it will surely come."

Line 19, *breathe . . . live*. Ezek. 37:9, from his vision of the resurrection of the dry
bones.

Line 22, *stop my ears*. Isa 33:15, "that stoppeth his ears from hearing of blood[shed]";
cf. Prov. 21:13.

against the scolding of the marketplace,
the terrible shrieks of the hawkers.
Only at times do I scream in rage,   25
and at once I rebuke myself for letting it happen:
loss of self-control.

I have to let go of it all,
to forbear winter and summer,
until that head breaks through and dawns, pearly,   30
tender, red.
No eye has ever beheld its like.

Rough Draft

Not to leave footprints
not to leave a trail of signs,
anyway I'm not going to stay in this place.
Not to write letters
not to collect souvenirs,   5
photographs,
not to arrange them in an album in marching order.
Not to collect documents,
not to gather in summer,
not whitewash, not remodel,   10
not settle down, not be a settler.
In the dark to withdraw from the moving caravan
perhaps after a grave illness
like Rachel. This business

Line 9, *gather in summer*. Prov. 10:5, "He that gathereth in summer is a wise son."

Line 11, *settle down . . . be a settler*. The biblical verb *le-hitnachel*, "to settle the land," acquired a specific political valence since 1967 in reference to the settlements in the Occupied Territories.

Line 14, *like Rachel*. The modernist poet Rachel [Bluvstein] (1890–1931), who died of tuberculosis. Born in Russia, Rachel was one of the first women poets to write in Hebrew in the pre-State Yishuv. See "Like Rachel."

has no dignity, no importance: 15
dust on the roads
rising up to the sky.
I have no need to arrive.

August 1983

Making a Living

To hell with the poem, I need 120 New Shekels.
And that's in response to what I heard from you
and I heard you
and I heard you and you and you.
For the sake of poesy   5
one says of the sea that it never rests.
But as for me, I never make it to the sea,
I shuffle along on the street
and I have no relief and you have no peace,
and the floor tiles are crooked   10
and that's the little I have to say,
in fact I've been silent for years
and I'm still saying nothing today,
and as for the splendor fretted with golden fire
I'd gladly forgo it all,   15
in fact, I can hardly recall it
which is quite a nuisance
and not just in the practical sense.
And whatever I've said is nothing but
a hurried groan and a clearing of the throat,   20
because to hell with the poem and all its rhymes.
I need 120 New Shekels,
that's the bottom line.

Line 1, *New Shekels*. NIS, New Israeli Shekel, the Israeli currency since 1985.

Lines 2–4, *you*. Addressees all feminine.

No Stitchery More Precise

Ido Awakes

Ido
with a clarion call arose:
suddenly awoke.
Tiny lion,
his sleep stole away.   5

In a trice he burst out crying.
Didn't really mean to annoy.
His sleep stole away.

Stretched out his hands.
Issued a command.   10
Sent for water,
some porridge or other,
nibbled a hanky,
banished the blankie.
Got good and mad,   15
sleep by now was not to be had.

*   *   *

Title, *Ido*. Ido Kalir, Ravikovitch's son, born in 1978.

Sweet baby,
what are you asking for?
A trifling matter:
Let all be done according to his word.   20

Suddenly he laughed,
remembered a sweet dream,
a tickle in the ribs.
Sweet baby.
For what did this baby try to do, after all?   25
drill into a mountain?
quarry boulders?

Sweet child,
whenever the spirit moves him
he smashes a pan or a spoon.   30
My love in the morning
my love in the evening,
my love all the livelong day.

March 1979

Little Child's Head

Things like that don't vex me anymore,
not the ways of wickedness nor the heart's folly
nor the prevailing blend
that has a bit of both.

The coarse ripples on the water grow calm.   5
No wind stirs the swamp of reeds.
A little child's head rests here on the pillow.
Deep in concentration, I see him.

Line 20, *according to his word.* A variation on the familiar blessing, thanking God for
a variety of foods: "Blessed art thou, O Lord our God, King of the Universe, by whose
word all things exist."

What passes between us, head to head,
before his eyelids close,   10
in the light of his lovely face, in the glance of an eye,
I dare not take upon my tongue.

No Stitchery More Precise

I gaze at the little one
and see the Flower of the Golden Heart lying on the pillow.
His mouth is open.
His eyes are finely drawn,
his head entrusted to sweet dreams.   5
Already he has sailed far beyond my reach.
The line of his brows like a taut canvas.
There is no stitchery more precise than this.

In Line at the Theater

Someday, perhaps, we may not recall
how we stood together in line,
your hand in mine.
And whenever you spoke to me
I couldn't hear a word   5
with all those mothers and children around.
And by the time I bent down to listen
you were already done.
We didn't manage to exchange a single sound.

Little one, have no fear,   10
stand right over here.

Line 2, *the Flower of the Golden Heart*. From a European folktale, beloved by Israeli
children, in which a magical flower is the only thing that can cure an ailing mother.

But you were afraid
and reached for my hand.
And the line! The line!
There was no way to get through that line.   15
And the fear was pooling in your eyes
and I was afraid you would burst into tears.
Suddenly you said, It's already four thirty.
I gasped: How on earth could it be four thirty?
And you grew rigid in your despair   20
and the line, the line stormed but didn't stir.
Little one,
your walnut eyes
were more than a mighty wind at my back.
I knew there would be no pleasure in store.   25
Then you said you don't wanna anymore.
Little one.
We went home in a cab the way rich people do.
In my hand, a pearl of great price.

The Glass Pavilion

Lemon tea
at the edge of the water,
lunch—a sandwich,
a slice of pie.
I could see you with my very own eyes.   5
All the walls were transparent glass.

I could say,
Ido, look!
See the water, how the ducks
are coming closer!   10
See, London,
the heart of the city,
look, a squirrel coming down from a tree.
Look at that lawn, what a bright color,
look, a swan somersaulting in the water,   15

look, a white one, look, a black.
That squirrel won't budge,
because of him you're afraid to cross.
Look over there: a dark red tree
and a greenish tree with a big fat trunk,   20
hard and bumpy
with a huge head of leaves.
Ido, look,
Ido, see:
The entire pavilion is made of glass.   25

June 1983

The Window

The Window

So what did I manage to do?
Me—for years I did nothing.
Just looked out the window.
Raindrops soaked into the lawn,
year in, year out.   5
That lawn was soft grass, high class.
Blackbirds strolled across it.
Later, tiny flowers blossomed, fine strings of beads,
most likely in spring.
Later tulips,   10
English daffodils,
snapdragons,
nothing special.
Me—I didn't do a thing.
Winter and summer revolved among blades of grass.   15
I slept as much as possible.
That window was as big as it needed to be.
Whatever was needed
I saw in that window.

Line 12, *snapdragons* (Heb. *lo'a ha-ari,* lit. "the lion's maw"). Ravikovitch uses a colloquial variant, *lo'a ha-arye,* also a Hebrew expression for living in a dangerous situation.

Birdy

This too shall be an ever-receding past
right now, around two in the morning,
middle of November, this torment
will turn into summer and winter and spring
in a perfect circle—   5
will become one memory, delicate, scorching,
twisted,
and even now I can see before my eyes
the corpse withering to dust
and from within it   10
rising as if from the ocean waves,
from out of a seashell,
a rosy naked new woman.
The present will become a chimera
as water turns into vapor.   15
And like a red pomegranate
my head will be filled with chimeras
filled with chimeras,
and drift in the lofty vault of the heavens
hollow and light,   20
dressed in feathers.

[Author's note.] Based on an American film of that title.

Title, *Birdy*. English title in the original. A 1984 film about a teenage boy obsessed
with birds as an escape from his grim life; after returning mute from the Vietnam war,
he is confined to an army mental hospital.

Finally I'm Talking

Yona, *shalom,*
this time I'm the one who's talking
and you won't interrupt anymore.
Now, God help us, you're in the ranks of the holy and pure.
Who would've believed you'd come to this,   5
that you'd finally calm down.
And what a riot you stirred up when you took your leave,
each man suddenly at his brother's throat. Hitting, spitting,
and instead of you, they hung on the wall
two drawings, that's all,   10
to help us recall.
And they called you holy and their faces grew pale,
and they called you defiled and oh how they sighed,
and they cried *Holy Holy, whore whore,*
and lots of sharp teeth tore the corpse limb from limb.   15
A sign you really were dead this time,
a quiet cadaver,
and now they're talking you up with feigned praise,
all those heirs you left behind,
you gave them free rein   20
but no restraint.
And whenever your name comes up there's a scandal,
fact or fiction, a tale to tell.
If you could only look, you would love it all,
but now, Yona, you're in an entirely novel condition,   25

Line 1, *Yona.* Yona Wallach (1944–1985), an important avant-garde feminist poet of
the 1970s and 1980s. The name Yona means "dove"; the poem presupposes the mean-
ing of dove in Jewish culture as a symbol of peace and of the soul. See "The Dove" and
"True Love Isn't What It Seems."

Line 1, *shalom.* Heb. "peace," also the common greeting for "hello" and "good-bye."

Line 4, *the holy and pure.* From the funeral prayer, *El Maleh Rachamim* ("O God Full
of Mercy"): "Grant . . . perfect rest beneath the shadow of thy divine presence, in the
exalted places among the holy and pure, who shine as the brightness of the firma-
ment." See "Requiem after Seventeen Years."

Line 7, *when you took your leave.* Wallach's dying of breast cancer became the occa-
sion for an extended, and at times raucous, public leave-taking.

Line 14, *Holy Holy.* Isa. 6:3.

you are one dead girl.
You're fading and coming closer, shape-shifting,
finally you're colorless, dove white.
An involuntary nobility oozes out of you.
All of a sudden you've got manners,   30
you've got inhibitions.
A good little girl from a proper home
knows to keep her mouth shut.
Doesn't utter a peep.

Yona, with all your antics and peculiar disposition,   35
your grand masquerades
and the show with its lifelong run,
you had a death that was beautiful, human, physical
and full of grace.

Hovering at a Low Altitude

I am not here.
I am on those craggy eastern hills
streaked with ice
where grass doesn't grow
and a sweeping shadow overruns the slope.   5
A little shepherd girl
with a herd of goats,
black goats,
emerges suddenly
from an unseen tent.   10
She won't live out the day, that girl,
in the pasture.

I am not here.
Inside the gaping mouth of the mountain
a red globe flares,   15

Title, *Hovering at a Low Altitude*. Israeli army language to describe helicopter patrols.
"To hover" (*le-rachef*) is also slang for "to stay cool, dissociated from the political
situation."

174

not yet a sun.
A lesion of frost, flushed and sickly,
revolves in that maw.

And the little one rose so early
to go to the pasture.   20
She doesn't walk with neck outstretched
and wanton glances.
She doesn't paint her eyes with kohl.
She doesn't ask, Whence cometh my help.

I am not here   25
I've been in the mountains many days now.
The light will not scorch me. The frost cannot touch me.
Nothing can amaze me now.
I've seen worse things in my life.

I tuck my dress tight around my legs and hover   30
very close to the ground.
What ever was she thinking, that girl?
Wild to look at, unwashed.
For a moment she crouches down.
Her cheeks soft silk,   35
frostbite on the back of her hand.
She seems distracted, but no,
in fact she's alert.
She still has a few hours left.
But that's hardly the object of my meditations.   40
My thoughts, soft as down, cushion me comfortably.
I've found a very simple method,
not so much as a foot-breadth on land

Lines 21–23, *neck outstretched . . . wanton glances . . . paint her eyes*. Negating Isa.
3:16 ff., Jer. 4:30, Ezek. 23:40, the prophets' denunciations of Zion as a whoring
woman.

Line 24, *Whence cometh my help*. Negating Psalm 121:1–2, "I will lift up mine eyes
unto the hills. From whence cometh my help? My help cometh from the Lord."

Line 43, *foot-breadth* (Heb. *midrakh kaf-regel*). Deut. 2:4–5, God enjoining the people
of Israel: "You are crossing into the territory of your brothers the sons of Esau, who
dwell in Seir. . . . Do not provoke them, for I shall not give you of their land, not so
much as a foot-breadth" (literal translation).

and not flying, either—
hovering at a low altitude.   45

But as day tends toward noon,
many hours
after sunrise,
that man makes his way up the mountain.
He looks innocent enough.   50
The girl is right there, near him,
not another soul around.
And if she runs for cover, or cries out—
there's no place to hide in the mountains.

I am not here.   55
I'm above those savage mountain ranges
in the farthest reaches of the East.
No need to elaborate.
With a single hurling thrust one can hover
and whirl about with the speed of the wind.   60
Can make a getaway and persuade myself:
I haven't seen a thing.
And the little one, her eyes start from their sockets,
her palate is dry as a potsherd,
when a hard hand grasps her hair, gripping her   65
without a shred of pity.

A Deadly Fear

Lying on her back.
Mattress, blanket, sheet and fever are her safety net.
Her smallness takes up a third of the bed
or even less,
a quarter of the blanket.   5
She is content.

Line 59, *hurling*. Isa. 22:17–18, lit. "Behold, the Lord will hurl you away . . . ; there
you will die." See "The Hurling."

Flings out one arm, both arms,
a gesture without substance,
without intention.
Her legs drawn up, muscles cramped. 10
They twitch and jerk. Sometimes
her stomach hurts her and then she cries
in a voice that rises and falls, rises and rises.
She begs for help, quick.
Can't budge. 15
Can't express herself
nor does she have thoughts that require expression.
If she doesn't get help right away
she thinks she will die.
She is certain 20
no human has ever known a fear like hers.
She must be loved without delay,
fed this very instant, handled with care.
She doesn't have a shred of patience,
doesn't trust the future. 25
She must be granted the right of way.
She's insanely afraid of abandonment.
A year or half a year from today,
she may attain the state of sitting upright,
she'll sprout up as if in gratitude. 30
Then cautiously, with great trepidation,
she'll concede a bit, one imperceptible concession,
and then another. Socialization
has an inescapable trajectory.
And sometimes, balky baby that she is, 35
she won't be able,
she won't be able to budge.
If they leave her alone
she feels she will die,
she feels something dreadful will happen. 40
They must hold onto me tight, she feels, or else
I die.

Line 42, *I die*. Rachel's plea to Jacob (Gen. 30:1): "Give me children, or else I die."

At Her Own Pace

A woman is holding a small photo.
She is no longer in her prime.
Travels a lot. Airplane. Suitcase.
For months on end, she stays
with relatives of hers.   5
"At your pace I couldn't," she says.
An introverted woman,
gentle in her ways.
People give in to her. She gives in too.
She's on the move again. Airplane. Suitcase.   10
Nothing was set in advance.
The phone rang. She was flooded with a joy
that could tear the heavens open. He's a man who's not hers
in the full sense of the word.

She walks from room to room alone. An endless calm.   15
In the innermost circle of her being, she's torn to pieces.
On the outside she's calm. Doesn't really seek
to take possession.
A small passport photo in her hand.
He's wearing a tie. A featureless face,   20
I would say. For her he's really
the world entire.
Apart from that, outside the innermost circle
she's calm and recoiling
at her own pace.   25

Cinderella in the Kitchen

The few good hours in Cinderella's day
were spent down there in the kitchen.
She had freedom of mind,
we may venture to say.
She pressed her hands to her temples,   5
her hair was all splattered with grease.

She went sailing off in her mind for distances
that cannot be measured,
cannot be explained,
sensations she knew but didn't name.   10
She lowered her eyes to her apron,
befouled and begrimed,
and knew what a great distance there lies
between X and Y,
if indeed it is subject to measure,   15
since what begins in the here and now
has no end in time
no point in time.
She drew a circle around herself,
made herself a sign,   20
just a make-believe line.
And she saw those two going out in their best attire,
elegant, glamorous, dripping perfumes,
their necks outstretched.
But she didn't really want to be in their shoes.   25
Her imagination was filled with infinite treasure,
truly infinite,
though formless, diffuse.
She had a tiny knot of heat in her throat
and a pounding heartbeat, fervid, sickly.   30
She was alone and apart,
weepy, feverish,
ready at any moment to quit living.
Her point of view
was uncommonly remote   35
as if she lived on Mars,
the planet of war.
And she clenched her fists and said:
I'm going off to war—

Then dozed off in bed.   40

Line 19, *drew a circle around herself.* Like Honi the Circle-Maker (*Honi Ha-Me'agel*),
who, according to rabbinic legend drew a magic circle around himself to pray for rain
(Mishnah *Ta'anit* 3:8); he is also said to have slept for seventy years.

Line 24, *their necks outstretched.* Isa. 3:16, from his condemnation of the whoring
daughters of Zion; see "Hovering at a Low Altitude."

Light and Darkness

If you can dim the light, madam,
if you focus the light with some wisdom,
he will surely be seen, that man,
from the window. That man
in the lofty window,   5
I cannot disclose which floor,
with layer upon layer of darkness beneath him.
That man doesn't sleep, to be sure.

And who is the speaker here?
A woman who doesn't know joy   10
as a natural state.
Who finds no favor in the mirror's eye,
who's not at ease.
Wears glasses,
can't handle details.   15

It's not by chance
that I sit so long in the dark,
dimming the lights,
leaving the corners in darkness.
In the dark I see her   20
sitting as I do.
She draws the shutters closed against me,
turns her back on me,
pretends to my face that she doesn't see,
knowing full well   25
every motion of hers is manifest to me.

And the man in the window,
a visitor from a distant land,
a man of means,
stays up all night.   30
Entertaining some woman
he has just met.

Soon he'll push aside the drapes,
survey his surroundings with satisfaction.
Before his eyes, a foreign city.   35
He's had his fill of foreign cities.
On his wrist, an accurate watch.
He knows that right now in the thick of night,
a woman sits unseen
in the dimmed lights.   40
She can see into his heart.
He can read her thoughts.
They share a kind of closeness
he'd better not put to the test of intimacy.
The two of them, compassed about in darkness   45
as in a blanket. Things are really good
between them.

We Had an Understanding

Savta, Grandma,
could it be our transparent skin,
skin that doesn't protect the flesh,
not in the least.
This story of ours   5
has details that are better left untold,
it's good to leave blots of forgetting upon things past.
But there is no question
of the resemblance between us
that begot understanding without any caring.   10

A Panama hat and a European lady's attire
before the bad times set in
and the rattan armchairs started falling apart.
You'd sometimes cook with a great to-do,
you never neglected to mention   15
how much trouble it was.

                *   *   *

Line 45, *compassed about*. Jonah 2:5: "The waters compassed me about."

And the days when you argued with the radio,
having it out with the exegetes
about the weekly Bible portion
with the Talmudic logic you'd learned from your grandpa.   20
Among the "Daughters of Zion" in that godforsaken Bialystok
there was no maiden as haughty as you
and even that had some measure of justification.
Savta, it's you I mean,
my European *savta*, not the other one.   25
I remember you once in a blue moon
or not so blue,
as in a closed chapter of a life,
with the intensity of a deep memory,
a dormant empathy.   30
Perhaps it's the transparent skin that unites us—
you without defenses
I without defenses.
None of this brought you any benefit
and you were always one to insist on benefits.   35
As for that ending, we'd better not talk about it.
Savta, that life finally came to an end,
which was also a kind of solution.
Now when you no longer have any daily needs
it might do you some good to know   40
we had an understanding.

Line 21, *Daughters of Zion* (Heb. *Bnot Tziyon*). A youth organization for girls in East-
ern Europe, affiliated with the centrist Socialist-Zionist *Po'aley Tziyon* ("Workers of
Zion") movement.

"And sympathy is all we need, my friend"

A human being hath shewed thee what is good
and what the Lord doth require of thee.
Leave the wondrous works to His palace.
Suffice it to say
a human being hath shewed thee what is good.   5
You are obligated to find the time, and that's that.
What does it mean, obligated?
Obligated.
Here to your right stands a human being,
still a boy.   10
Like you, he's got problems making a living,
and with identity too.

At night he's choking
with anxiety, not pulmonary insufficiency.
How they torment themselves with the need for friendship,   15
obligatory friendship,
these boys with their severe faces.
And so skinny too,
if I were their mother
I'd no doubt be one gloomy woman.   20

What's there to say?
Everybody's thirsty for love,
what a humiliating business it is
to be so vulnerable.
But I have the audacity to say: 25

Title, *"And sympathy . . . friend"* (English title in the original). Paraphrasing a line of "Sympathy," a 1970 song by the British rock band Rare Bird.

Lines 1–2, *A human being hath shewed . . . require of thee.* Micah 6:8, "He hath shewed thee, O man, what is good; and what doth the Lord require of thee, but to do justly, and to love mercy, and to walk humbly with thy God?" Ravikovitch reads this verse in accord with modern Hebrew usage, taking *adam*, "human being," as the subject rather than the object of address.

Line 3, *wondrous works.* Job 37:16, "Dost thou know . . . the wondrous works of him who is perfect in knowledge?"

Everyone's thirsty for love
and whoever won't pour a glass of water for the thirsty
is doomed to gag on his own spit
to the end of his days.

A Declaration for the Future

A person, when he's hungry
or insecure,
will make compromises,
do things he never dreamt of in his life.

Suddenly he's got a crooked back,   5
and what happened to his back
that it got so crooked?
Loss of pride.
And his smile is frozen
and both hands filthy,   10
or so it seems to him,
from coming in contact
with moist objects
whose touch he cannot escape.

And he has no choice,   15
or so it seems to him,
and it's a marvel
how for years he'll forbear,
and merely record
the annals of his life   20
within,
year after year.

February 1986

The Law of Gravitation

In the dark movie theater
two people who knew each other to a limited degree
were sitting
and their heads reached the point of contact.
And it wasn't the hand of chance.   5
Hardly the hand of chance.
He acknowledged her presence,
she was not indifferent to his.
Shades of *Take me under thy wing,*
and she in her heart: "You take me under yours."   10
No thunder and lightning between them,
just the beginning
of a tectonic shift, clandestine, subversive.
She sensed it distinctly, without a doubt.
She sensed surprise.   15
Got up and went out.

February 1986

Gadi in Richmond

On the wooden bench in the park he told me:
I'm afraid to die, even when I get old.
I don't know what it will be like.
How can I know what it will be like?

And I said, It won't be so bad,   5
it might even be with the kiss of God.

Line 9, *Take me under thy wing.* From a well-known love poem of that name by Bialik: "Take me under thy wing, / Be thou a mother and a sister unto me."

Line 6, *the kiss of God* (Heb. *mitat neshika*, lit. "death-by-kiss"). According to rabbinic lore, the righteous die a painless death when God kisses them on the mouth.

Then the Coca-Cola spilled
and he laughed and laughed, he couldn't stop.
He clapped me on the back, really hard,
like a man whose virility bursts from his body.   10

Then he ran over to the deserted pier
and posed intrepid for a photo op with the geese.
He climbed down the short ladder to the water
and I held my breath in terror.

The water turned gray under the cumulus clouds   15
and green at its edge under weeping branches.
Later on, night made the water turn black,
the sky darkened, the river grew dark.
A formation of low-flying airplanes zoomed over us,
all of them headed west.   20

Calm and clumsy, the great round globe
rolled westward too.
Then Gadi began to laugh again
because the Coke that spilled
got all over his clothes.   25

For the Ascent of His Soul

He's dead and buried.
Dead and buried, that's that.
Dead. That's a fact.
I had a kind of story with him
once upon a time,   5
not really a story,
just some thing that happened.
The pupils of his eyes were translucent,
his back was bent,

Title, *For the Ascent of His Soul* (Heb. *le-iluy nishmato*). A prayer for the soul of the
deceased to rise up to heaven.

even without me he had enough trouble.   10
I came to him on a Shabbat,
which Shabbat?
a seething hot Shabbat.
Jasmine in bloom,
wolf's milk growing wild,   15
you name it, dearie,
all blooming in that garden.
(The garden wasn't his.)
He had a roommate,
no assets to his name.   20
Flat broke, to boot.
So I came that Shabbat afternoon,
everything was set
for the chiming of the spheres.
I said I was on my way,   25
couldn't stick around,
had some other plans for the day.
He got desperate.
Didn't hide his despair.
Said, What will I do now?   30
And I thought: What will he do?
Let him do whatever he wants.
Anyway, what did I ever do to him?

In time, I saw what I did to him.
Love spurned was the very worst   35
of whatever befell me.
All that in good time.
Meanwhile, he got himself a wife,
sired sons,
put down roots.   40
The years passed over us all,
flying in low formation;
people were shot in the back, in the head.
He wasn't hit.
And now he's buried and dead,   45
dug under and covered up,
and there's no end
but that end.

True Love Isn't What It Seems

Everybody loved Yona,
everybody in the room loved Yona,
and whenever the talk turned to books,
they'd say: Oh that Yona, may she rest in peace,
but the memory of Yona was dwindling fast   5
for perhaps we didn't truly love her.
It's natural for memory to be gnawed to shreds
just as the earth gnaws away at a corpse.
The question is, Do we love our friends?
No, we don't really love our friends.   10
But do we love our children?
Sometimes we do love our children,
but that too, by and large, only to a limited extent,
the way the orange tree loves the orange.
The rest is a range of misunderstandings   15
and all of these eat away at true love,
with a greedy mouth.
The question is, Do we really love ourselves
even as Jonathan loved David?
It's best that we speak words of truth,   20
not like David's lament for Jonathan.
Ourselves we love with great devotion,
attuned to ourselves with rapt attention.
And even that amounts to a real improvement,
for just a few months ago   25
our body was seized by a powerful yearning
to hurl itself urgently from the roof.

Line 1, *Yona*. Feminist poet Yona Wallach (1944–1985). See "Finally I'm Talking."

Line 17, *with a greedy mouth*. See "Like Rachel."

Line 19, *even as Jonathan loved David*. "The soul of Jonathan was knit with the soul of David, and Jonathan loved him as his own soul" (1 Sam. 18:1–3).

Line 21, *David's lament*. 2 Sam. 1:19–27, a politically expedient lament on the death of Saul and Jonathan.

ॐ

A Jewish Portrait

She
is not your sort.
She's a Diaspora kind of Jew whose eyes dart around
in fear.
Wears an old-fashioned dress,   5
her hair pulled back without a bit of grace.
Doesn't undo her bundles.
Why should she undo her bundles?
Any place she might stumble on
is a place that won't last.   10
Her bed is unmade.
No sense adorning what will not last.

On the road.
Caravans pass her by,
Ukrainian peasants in their carts   15
and dark-skinned refugees, screaming;
babes in arms dry up in the sun,
flies clinging to their eyes.

Title, *A Jewish Portrait* (Heb. *dyokan yehudi*). Means both "Portrait of a Jew" and "Portrait in the Jewish Style"—an ambiguity, sustained throughout the poem, blurring the distinction between Diaspora Jew and Palestinian refugee.

Line 3, *a Diaspora kind of Jew* (Heb. *yehudiya galutit*). Reappropriating the derogatory Israeli stereotype about Jews with an Eastern European "ghetto" mentality; the adjective *galutit* can be applied to an Israeli who behaves "like a Jew from the Diaspora."

People carry mattresses on their heads,
a clangor of pots and pans.   20
People curse her as she goes by:
She's slow,
slowing down the caravan.

She goes off to the side of the road and stops.
She has no baby,   25
can wait for dark.

Suddenly, she sees a coin in the dust—a spark.
She smiles an inward smile.
In her mind's eye
rivulets well up in the thicket.   30
It's wrong to think she has lost her mind.
A kernel of sun-crimson dawns in her heart.
There. She's no longer upset.

She has no use for this business, Jerusalem.
Day after day they wrangle over the Temple Mount,   35
each man smites and reviles his brother,
and the dead prophet shrieks,
Who hath required this at your hand, to trample My courts?

Once the caravan has crossed,
night will fall and she'll find her house.   40
Her feet stub against the sharp gravel-stones,
dust soils her dress.
She will bolt the inner door,
pull the shutters closed around her.
Only the soles of her feet will she bathe,   45
so boundless her weariness.
In the dark she knows the features of her face
as a blind man knows the feel of his temples.
Her eyes are the blue eyes of Khazars,

Line 38, *Who hath required . . . courts?* Quoting Isa. 1:12, a condemnation of empty piety that masks unethical conduct.

Line 49, *Khazars.* A Turkic people from Central Asia, commonly believed to have converted to Judaism in the Middle Ages.

her face a broad face,   50
her body the heavy body of a native woman,
third generation in the Land of Israel.

June 4, 1982

They're Freezing Up North

in memory of Baruch Kurzweil

He gets up, walks, stands still, drops dead,
the father of some other woman.
Flicks out a long tongue from a better world,
quick as an acrobat
eerie as a demon.   5
Most of that history
I didn't know, didn't see.

And now in winter it's very cold here,
for some other woman, not me.
Up North babies are freezing right now,   10
whoever wasn't thrown into the pit,
whoever the bullets didn't hit,
gets tormented some other way.
It's so cold in the North,
the Near North.   15

I want to tell him all about it.
He was a good man

Line 51, *native* (Heb. *mi-bney ha-makom*). Official code for Israeli Palestinians.

[Author's note.] During the first winter after the war in Lebanon broke out, tents were distributed to refugees whose houses were destroyed. Some Palestinian women set fire to the tents, which in any case provided no shelter from the rain and the chill of a Lebanese winter.

Epigraph, *Baruch Kurzweil* (1907–1972). Professor of Hebrew and World Literature at Bar-Ilan University; an influential literary critic during the 1950s and 1960s. Raviko-vitch's mentor and one of the first to support her literary efforts; see introduction. Died by suicide.

before he died what you might call
an unnatural death.
If the earth had been given into his hand   20
he would've brandished an old-fashioned sword,
and just to play it safe
pressed his hand, perhaps, to his heart.
He never would've let them start.

Who was he, what was he?   25
A father and master, one might say.
He stands up, falls down, passes away,
chooses to collapse then and there in slo-mo
with a joke about escorting the Sabbath Queen
after Havdalah to the Feast of the Just.   30
Beyond all this,
appalling pain.

What do I need them all for,
thinking about them all,
remembering them all?   35
Babies are freezing
in the slanted lashings of the rain.
Mothers are burning
their canvas tents
to make a nice little bonfire in winter.   40
He stands up, passes on and he's free.
This bloody mess
is all on my head now,
all on me.

Early November 1982

Line 20, *If the earth . . . his hand.* "The earth is given into the hand of the wicked" (Job 9:24). An implied contrast between Kurzweil's courtly conservatism and that of Ariel Sharon, who directed the 1982 Lebanon invasion.

Line 29, *Sabbath Queen* (Heb. *Shabbat ha-Malka*). Traditional way of referring to the Sabbath. With the final meal of the Sabbath, the *Melaveh Malka,* the Sabbath is "escorted" as she departs. Ravikovitch recalls in a 1980 essay that Kurzweil would customarily invite students to his house for the *Melaveh Malka* meal.

Line 30, *Havdalah.* A ritual marking the end of the Sabbath and the beginning of the work week. *the Feast of the Just* (Heb. *se'udat tzadikim*). A banquet for righteous souls in Paradise.

You Can't Kill a Baby Twice

By the wastewaters of Sabra and Shatila,
there you transported human beings, respectable
quantities of human beings,
from the animal kingdom
to kingdom come.   5

Night after night.
First they shot
then hanged the lot,
the rest they butchered with knives.
Terror-struck women scrambled up, frantic,   10
on a mound of earth:
"They're butchering us down there,
in Shatila."

A thin tail of newborn moon was hanging
over the camps.   15
Our own soldiers lit up the place with searchlights
till it was bright as day.
"Back to the camp, *marsch!*" the soldier commanded
the shrieking women of Sabra and Shatila.
After all, he had his orders.   20
And the kids were already laid out in the fetid waters,
their mouths gaping,
at peace.
No one will harm them now.
You can't kill a baby twice.   25

And the moon's tail grew fuller and fuller
till it turned into a talent of gold.

                     ※   ※   ※

Lines 1–2, *By the wastewaters . . . there.* Cf. Psalm 137:1, "By the rivers of Babylon,
there we sat down, yea, we wept, when we remembered Zion." See "*Adloyada* in
Manhattan."

Line 18, *marsch.* Ravikovitch uses the German imperative verb here.

Line 27, *talent of gold* (Heb. *kikar zahav*). A heavy round of precious metal; a biblical
measure.

Those sweet soldiers of ours,
there was nothing in it for them.
Their one and only desire   30
was to come home in peace.

Get Out of Beirut

Take the knapsacks,
the clay jugs, the washtubs,
the Korans,
the battle fatigues,
the bravado, the broken soul,   5
and what's left in the street, a little bread or meat,
and kids running around like chickens in the heat.
How many children do you have?
How many children did you have?
It's hard to keep the children safe in times like these.   10

Not the way it used to be in the old country,
in the shade of the mosque, under the fig tree,
where you'd get the kids out of the house in the morning
and tuck them into bed at night.

Whatever's not fragile, gather up in those sacks: 15
clothing, bedding, blankets, diapers,
some memento, perhaps,
a shiny artillery shell,
or a tool that has practical value,
and the babies with pus in their eyes   20

Line 31, *to come home in peace*. From the popular 1967 song about a decorated sol-
dier *Giva't Ha-Tachmoshet* ("Ammunition Hill"), now quoted sarcastically in antiwar
discourse.

Title, *Get Out of Beirut*. Slogan of Israeli antiwar demonstrators during the siege of
Beirut and of the adjacent Palestinian refugee camps in the 1982 war.

and the RPG kids.
We'd love to see you afloat in the water with no place to go
no port and no shore.
You won't be welcome anywhere.
You're human beings who were thrown out the door,   25
you're people who don't count anymore.
You're human beings that nobody needs.
You're a bunch of lice
crawling about
that pester and bite   30
till we all go nuts.

Beheaded Heifer

Took another step,
then a few steps more.
His glasses dropped,
his yarmulke dropped.
Took another step   5
drenched in blood,
dragging his feet.
Ten steps more
and he's not a Jew
not an Arab anymore—   10
disembodied.

*   *   *

Line 21, *RPG kids.* Youngest members of the PLO, who used rocket-propelled grenades (RPGs).

Title, *Beheaded Heifer.* "If one be found slain in the field, and it be not known who hath slain him, the elders of [the nearest] city shall take an heifer, and shall strike off the heifer's neck. And all the elders of that city shall wash their hands over the heifer and say, 'Our hands have not shed this blood.' And the blood shall be forgiven them" (Deut. 21:1–9, abridged). Cf. also Num. 19 on rites of expiation. According to Ravikovitch, this poem is based on an actual incident in which a yeshiva student was shot in the Hebron marketplace and left to die because no one knew his identity; the Israelis assumed he was a Palestinian, and the Palestinians—an Israeli.

God-awful uproar; people shrieking, Why are you murdering us?
Others scuttering about,
rushing to exact revenge.

He lies gasping on the ground, a death rattle,   15
a body torn open,
and the blood spilling out of the flesh.
The blood spilling out of the flesh.

He died here or there
—some degree of uncertainty remains.   20
What do we know for a fact?
"One found slain in the field."

It is said, Suffering cleanseth sin,
man is like dust in the wind,
but who was that man   25
lying there lonely,
choking on his blood?
What did he see
what did he hear
in the uproar that seethed   30
above him?
It is also said,
If thou seest even thine enemy's ass
lying under its burden,
thou shalt surely help.   35

If one be found slain in the field
if one be found slain on the ground,
let your elders go out and slaughter a heifer
and scatter its ashes in the stream.

Lines 33–35, *thine enemy's ass . . . surely help.* Exod. 23:5, which enjoins one to help
even an enemy; see "Six Hundred Thirteen Commandments Plus One."

On the Attitude toward Children
in Times of War

He who destroys thirty babies
it is as if he'd destroyed three hundred babies,
and toddlers too,
or even eight-and-a-half-year-olds;
in a year, God willing, they'd be soldiers   5
in the Palestine Liberation Army.

Benighted children,
at their age
they don't even have a real worldview.
And their future is shrouded too: 10
refugee shacks, unwashed faces,
sewage flowing in the streets,
infected eyes,
a negative outlook on life.

And thus began the flight from city to village,   15
from village to burrows in the hills.
As when a man did flee from a lion,
as when he did flee from a bear,
as when he did flee from a cannon,
from an airplane, from our own troops.   20

He who destroys thirty babies,
it is as if he'd destroyed one thousand and thirty,
or one thousand and seventy,

[Author's note.] This is a variation on a poem by Natan Zach that deals [satirically]
with the question of whether there were exaggerations in the number of children
reported killed in the [1982] Lebanon War.

Lines 1–2, *He who destroys . . . babies.* Cf. Babylonian Talmud, *Sanhedrin* 4:5: "He
who destroys a single human soul . . . , it is as if he had destroyed an entire world."

Lines 17–18, *As when a man . . . bear.* Amos 5:19, about the danger of apocalyptic
yearnings.

thousand upon thousand.
And for that alone shall he find   25
no peace.

Two Isles Hath New Zealand

Africa's not the place to go right now.
Plagues, famine—the human body can't bear it.
Brutality. They flog human beings with bullwhips.
Asia—it would make your hair stand on end.
Trapped in the mountains, trapped in the swamps.   5
The human body can't bear it,
there are limits to the life force, after all.

As for me,
He shall make me to lie down in green pastures
in New Zealand.   10

Over there, sheep with soft wool,
the softest of wools,
graze in the meadow.
Truehearted folk herd their flocks,
on Sundays they pay a visit to church   15
dressed in sedate attire.

No point hiding it any longer:
We're an experiment that went awry,
a plan that misfired,
tied up with too much murderousness.   20
Why should I care about this camp or that,
screaming till their throats are raw,

Lines 9, 29, *green pastures, still waters*. Psalm 23.

Line 10, *New Zealand*. In contemporary Hebrew, a place of ultimate escape.

Line 14, *Truehearted folk*, and line 30, *kindhearted folk*. Ironically invoking the Christian settlers' massacre of the aboriginal Maoris.

splitting fine hairs.
In any case, too much murderousness.
To Africa I'm not going   25
and not to Asia, either.
I'm not going anyplace.

In New Zealand
in green pastures, beside the still waters,
kindhearted folk   30
will share their bread with me.

Hamlet, Supreme Commander

My protest is not in bitterness.
It is a cat's paw. At its tips are claws.
A puny complaint is naught but the whimper of a cooing infant,
drowned out in the din.
Too long have we bemoaned the soul's suffering   5
with the muted meekness of the weak.
For who would bear the whips and scorns of time,
The oppressor's wrong, the proud man's contumely,
The insolence of office, and the spurns
That patient merit of th'unworthy takes   10
without growing—sedulous, in secret—
a nail sharp-whetted as a cat's paw
to wipe out with one swift swipe of the hand
that affront.

[Author's note.] Lines 7–10 are quoted from Avraham Shlonsky's [Hebrew] translation of *Hamlet* [III.i.71–2, 74–5; the only line omitted, tellingly, is III.i.73: "The pangs of despis'd love, the law's delay."]

MOTHER

AND

CHILD

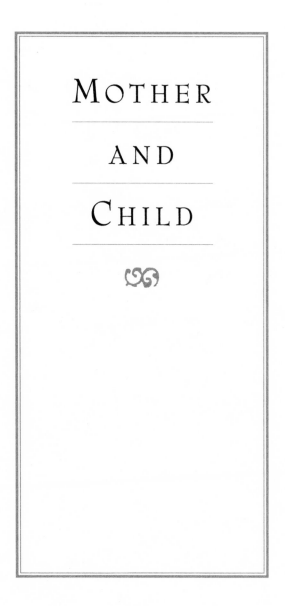

Atypical Autumn

Little by little I get a clearer picture
of how I got trapped here.
Ten in the morning, after a sleepless night
—this bucolic tranquillity.
Potted plants in bloom wherever the eye comes to rest.   5
Handwoven runners on every conceivable surface
and the teakettle
and the conspicuous paucity of houseware,
the tranquillity within,
and from without, the voice of a sulky toddler.   10
They took his swing.

Someone is digging with a simple farm implement,
I forgot what it's called.
(Forgot? Never mind.)
A rhythmic thumping, the whoosh of a hose dragged along.   15
Everyone here is raking and cultivating
the fauna and the flora.
The women also knit quite a bit;
manual labor stands at the very top
of the ladder here.   20
This diligence and the urge to be of use
beget an illusion of the idyllic.
If not for their terror of Labor Movement values,
every man would swallow his friend alive.

Three days now my mother's been sleeping the sleep of the just.   25
I told Ido: *Savta* is sleeping in peace and quiet.
And Ido said: Maybe that's sleep everlasting?
God forbid, I told him,
not sleep everlasting,
just peace and quiet.   30

Lines 23–24, *If not for . . . swallow . . . alive.* Cf. *Pirkey Avot* (Ethics of the Fathers)
3:2, lit. "Pray for the welfare/peace of the regime (Heb. *shloma shel malkhut*); but for
the fear thereof, men would swallow each other alive."

And yet, without sowing alarm,
I tell myself
sleep everlasting is the best sleep of all.

Attempt to Express an Opinion

Rain on the piazza
of Santa Maria Novella.
A few people with umbrellas,
a drizzle of rain, very light.
And I am thinking: 5
What is the meaning of the word "banal"?
Have I fathomed your opinion,
have I had an opinion at all?
Rain on Piazza Santa Maria
and rain on Piazza Santa Croce   10
and rain shedding its drops on the city floor
and all over Tuscany, etc.
And what little of this will stick to me
and what little of this will actually stay with me,
because most things   15
actually most things,
are just seeming, not actual being.
A drizzle of rain, very light,
moistens the cobblestones just a bit,
won't keep anyone off the street,   20
won't leave a sticky wetness.
Have I expounded to your satisfaction
my opinion about the banal,
have I fathomed your opinion
or have I expressed an opinion at all?   25

May 3, 1987

A Far-Reaching Athletic Exercise

Of all people,
that I should be out there swimming.
The waves have covered my shoulders
three days now;
I rise and fall, rise and fall   5
with the upper half of my body,
I've almost turned into some kind of boat.
And what of it? I won't turn into a fish, after all.
I propel myself forward like a guided object
down the Mediterranean, bearing slightly north,   10
in accord with the currents and coastlines.
Back in the Aegean, I met with heavy storms.
I had to go around in circles;
to all appearances
I was borne upon the waters like a log.   15
But in fact, I have absolute control over myself,
free from physical limitations,
filled with unswerving determination.
Legs, arms, arms-and-legs:
That's me.   20
On the first day I covered only an eighth of the distance,
my day went dark while I was still in the water,
but given my unusual condition
I had no problem to keep on propelling.
On the second day I was close to the breaking point;   25
my arms continued to propel me as before
but my willpower began to grow shaky.
I thought, after all this,
perhaps I won't even find land at the other end,

Line 7, *turned into some kind of boat*. See "Many Waters," where the speaker becomes
the sinking ship *Dahlia Maria*.

Line 8, *turn into a fish*. Cf. chapter 2 of David Grossman's novel *See Under: Love*
(1986), told from the point of view of a fish-like creature, Yam, a female reincarnation
of the ancient Near Eastern sea deity.

Line 23, *my unusual condition*. Cf. Yam's description of her predicament in *See Under:
Love*.

not real land, as when the ship's lookout proclaims: 30
Land ahoy!
All the same, I continued to rise and fall
with measured exertions
so as not to exhaust my resources.
By the third day I'd reached the middle of the sea,   35
I could no longer sense the heat of the waters or their chill.
My skin was wrinkled, its protective layer gone;
my hair was sticky and stiff.
I had three days' worth of propelling left
if the sea continued calm and clear,   40
but if it began to rage
there was no telling how long.
By then, I already knew I would make it,
that is, I would make it all the way to shore.
In an indeterminate physical condition   45
but without danger of substantial injury.
It's likely my skin will be shriveled and blistered;
for a few days I won't be able to look in the mirror.
My body rising stooped from the sea
may scare the life out of any passerby   50
who gives it half an eye.
On second glance,
what ever possessed me to embark on this swim,
which in any case has no end
but self-delusion.   55

Do or Die

Nights he would get roaring drunk,
spilling his glass, spattering the table;
sometimes he'd yell: Enough of this babble!
Flailing his arms around, searching for words
(now I've forgotten what it was all about,   5
whatever it was that got stuck in my mind).

    *   *   *

It seems he specialized in death as a subject,
he saw his years lined up in orderly columns,
twenty years, twenty-five years,
he knew that story was exhausting itself,   *10*
would break no records, would reach no heights,
he'd slough off his years like rotten teeth.
He would bang on the table, shatter some plate,
whatever stood in his way he would smash—
twenty years, twenty-five years,   *15*
he couldn't pull himself out of despair.
He was a man of little faith.
Heroic epics were not his forte,
he wouldn't even pick up the Bible.
His pittance of insight came via negation.   *20*
This is no tale of the hope for redemption.
He saw his shuffling life for what it was,
laid out before him, dwindling away,
plain as a jar of pickled turnips,
till death by natural causes, sudden or protracted.   *25*
But suddenly he was struck by a pang of empathy
and that was his profit for all his toil.
In the end he was buried in a potter's field
and that was his portion for all his toil.
Thus in his beginning he foresaw his end,   *30*
a life no worse than any other,
a common death and a hasty funeral.

Signs and Portents

When a glass drops,
a chip darts,
a scrap of paper slips
and something stirs or starts

Lines 27, 29, *profit, portion*. Eccl. 3:9, "What profit hath he that worketh in that
wherein he laboreth?" and Eccl. 2:10, "and this was my portion of all my labor."

out of bounds,   5
one had better beware.

Now I write, now I stop,
big deal, one might think
a wad of paper got stuck in my throat.
I'm no longer I, so to speak.   10
Half an I, and diminishing fast.
A stirring in the air. The matrix doesn't hold.
Perhaps I'm the one who is falling fast.

And I refuse to believe,
I absolutely refuse to see.   15

The Cat

Ido told me: Some workers are busy outside
and I leaned out and saw: A cat just went by.
A portly cat, speckled gray and orange,
an unusual combination.
Passed among stinging nettles,   5
swiftly vanished,
slipped away.
The margosa tree with its scrawny trunk
and dark green leaves.
An unhistoric morning   10
within the borders of house and yard.
Something like a light wind hovering among the leaves.
The yard on its eastern front already sunk in shadow.
From my place I could clearly see
the meager decor in the flat across the way.   15
We are all of us mute.
That cat saved my life.

Line 7, *slipped away* (Heb. *chamak avar*). Song of Songs 5:6.
Line 8, *margosa* (Heb. *izdarekhet*). See "Even for a Thousand Years."
Line 12, *wind hovering*. Cf. Gen. 1:2. See "The Finish Line."

State of Alert Drill

Let me tell you the truth:
It's possible to make do
with so-and-so many corners to a room,
color coordinated, pink, red, dark green,
with a delicate lace curtain   5
on the small melancholy window,
and a sense of consensual intimacy
between these objects
although they retain their estrangement.
And that's what there is in the room.   10
On the face of it, how little all that amounts to,
it's not even the little that contains the all,
but whatever's in plain sight is what there is.

There are things I keep hidden inside me
to baffle the eye of others.   15

And here I wait, wait unwearied,
with an obstinacy that has no basis,
to hear this is all just a drill in conserving energy
and preserving the state of readiness.

Poem in the Arab Style, Perhaps

Lesions of mildew creep up the shower curtain.
Come, my dear, what are you doing here?
Even the smallest thread on the floor can rob me of rest.
No way to maintain a sense of order.
Just patches of shadow under the table   5
aslant,
bold shadow on pale shadow, set in a square frame.
Oh, my dear, don't let these things be trifling in your eyes,

Line 12, *the little that contains the all*. Rabbinic concept; a microcosm.

though they're hardly grand, to be sure.
Even the eye seeks rest,   *10*
wants recompense for its toil.
The arabesques of the window bars
in repeating patterns, circle and line
—the blacksmith sought to invest them with beauty and form.
Beyond the square of shadow, the floor   *15*
reveals its defects,
the defects are right there before you,
and that's what disturbs the eye,
dispels any rest.
At the mouth of the large urn, inside the shadows of night, *20*
spectral images arise.
Come, my dear, what are you doing here?
What are you doing here beside me
when everyone's asleep?

Lying upon the Waters

Stinking Mediterranean city
stretched out over the waters
head between her knees,
her body befouled with smoke and dunghills.
Who will raise from the dunghills   *5*
a rotten Mediterranean city,
her feet scabby and galled?
Her sons requite each other
with knives.

*   *   *

Line 1, *Mediterranean city*. Tel Aviv, Israel's largest city, where Ravikovitch lived for much of her adult life.

Lines 2–3, *stretched out over* (Heb. *gahara*) . . . *her knees*. Inverts the biblical image of the prophets Elijah (1 Kings 17:21) and Elisha (2 Kings 4:34), each stretched out over a dead child to revive him. Cf. also 1 Kings 18:42.

Line 5, *Who will raise from the dunghills*. Calling into question Psalm 113:7, "He . . . lifteth the needy out of the dunghill."

Now the city is flooded with crates of plums and grapes,   *10*
cherries laid out in the marketplace
in sight of every passerby,
the setting sun peachy pink.
Who could really hate
a doped-up Mediterranean city   *15*
lowing like a cow in heat,
her walls Italian marble and crumbling sand,
decked out in rags and broidered work.
But she doesn't mean it at all,
doesn't mean anything at all.   *20*
And the sea is full, brimming at her blind forehead,
and the sun pours his horn of mercy upon her
when at dusk his wrath subsides.
And the squashes and cucumbers and lemons bursting
with color and juice   *25*
waft over her the sweet savor of summer perfumes.
And she is not worthy.
Not worthy of love or pity.

Filthy Mediterrean city,
how my soul is bound up with her soul.   *30*
Because of a lifetime,
an entire lifetime.

Line 12, *every passerby.* Ezek. 5:14, "I will make thee . . . a reproach among the nations . . . in the sight of all that pass by."

Line 18, *broidered work.* Ezek. 16:10, to the unfaithful Zion: "I clothed thee also with broidered work."

Line 30, *bound up with her soul.* cf. 1 Sam. 18:1, "the soul of Jonathan was knit with the soul of David." See "True Love Isn't What It Seems."

But She Had a Son

for Rachel Melamed-Eitan

An acquaintance that began midwinter
ripened by the end of spring.
A kindly woman, conciliatory.
She had a son,
a fallen soldier.   5
She bakes and cooks
part-time for City Hall.
A hot lunch is always ready on the table.
All this in an absolute refusal
to adjust.   10

In her own way, as if unperturbed,
she can stop the world short.
It's hard to know what she might do.
Without putting it into words,
she stakes her claim.   15
Didn't they take away her son?
No way will she see any justice at all
in that taking.
And who would dare tell her:
Come, wash your face, it's time,   20
be strong,
whatever happened, happened.

She sets out on an arduous journey,
a circular journey, to and fro.
With her own hands she heaps coals of fire beneath her,   25
deliberately strews the embers over her body.
She is Rachel. Which Rachel?
The one who had a son.
And she tells him night and day,

Epigraph, *Rachel Melamed-Eitan*. Mother of an army officer, Eitan Melamed, killed in August 1985; see "What a Time She Had!" After his death, she published two books of poems in his memory, coedited by Ravikovitch.

Line 25, *heaps coals of fire*. Prov. 25:22. See "The Dress."

summer and winter, feast day and holiday: 30
I am Rachel your mother
of clear mind and free will,
I will not be comforted.

What a Time She Had!

How did that story go?
As a rule she wouldn't have remembered so quickly.
In that soil no vineyard would grow.
A citrus grove stood there,
sickly,   5
stunted.
The single walnut tree blooming there bore no fruit
as if some essential life-giving element
were lacking in that soil.
Hard green lemons.   10
A balding patch of lawn.
A great tranquillity.
On the western side, the hedge went wild
and there was a honeysucker, of course
(today we'd call it a sunbird)   15
—if he were still alive
he'd be twenty years old.

In the valley, the army was hunting down human beings.
Fire in the thicket.
Summer's hellfire blazing as usual.   20
Evening mowing down shadows, merciless.

Line 31, *Rachel your mother*. Cf. Jer. 31:15, "Rachel, weeping for her children, refused to be comforted for her children, because they were not." Poem reverses the traditional interpretation, based on Jeremiah, according to which the matriarch Rachel becomes a metaphor for the nation. See "Lullaby"; cf. "Like Rachel" and "Rough Draft."

Line 12, *A great tranquillity*. From the title of a 1980 book of poems by Yehuda Amichai.

They sang her the songs of Zion
between one death and the next.
She wouldn't lay her head down
before the first light of day,   25
the first birdcall.
She herself died three or four times
in the course of those years.
Not an absolute and lasting death
but a kind of ongoing death agony.   30
A great yearning took hold of her in the lap of night,
powerful soulquakes.

The years have a way of begetting changes,
mysterious, cryptic.
She had no trouble remembering that story.   35
What a time she had!
Too bad that, so close to the ending,
she suddenly lost the ability
to stay alive.

A Mother Walks Around

A mother walks around with a child dead in her belly.
This child hasn't been born yet.
When his time is up the dead child will be born
head first, then trunk and buttocks
and he won't wave his arms about or cry his first cry   5
and they won't slap his bottom
won't put drops in his eyes
won't swaddle him
after washing the body.
He will not resemble a living child.   10
His mother will not be calm and proud after giving birth

Line 22, *the songs of Zion*. Psalm 137:3, "Sing us one of the songs of Zion." See "The
Captors Require a Song" and "Lullaby."

and she won't be troubled about his future,
won't worry how in the world to support him
and does she have enough milk
and does she have enough clothing   15
and how will she ever fit one more cradle into the room.
The child is a perfect *tzadik* already,
unmade ere he was ever made.
And he'll have his own little grave at the edge of the cemetery
and a little memorial day   20
and there won't be much to remember him by.
These are the chronicles of the child
who was killed in his mother's belly
in the month of January, in the year 1988,
"under circumstances relating to state security."   25

A Bottle on the Waters

Whatever I send out of this house
I cast away like a letter in a bottle.
Let it go forth from this place
and stand before you,
let it stand in my stead   5

Line 17, *tzadik*. A saintly Jew, used here about the Palestinian fetus.

Line 18, *unmade ere he was ever made*. Alluding to the hymn *Adon Olam* ("Master of the Universe"), where God is described as reigning "before any creature came to be made."

Title, *A Bottle on the Waters*. Osip Mandelstam famously wrote about the poet and his audience: "To whom then does the poet speak?" "[A] seafarer tosses a sealed bottle into the ocean waves. . . . Wandering along the dunes many years later, I happen upon it in the sand. I read the message, . . . the last will and testament of one who has passed on. . . . The message in the bottle was addressed to its finder. I found it. . . . I have become its secret addressee." ("On the Addressee," trans. Jane Gary Harris and Constance Link). Echoing Mandelstam, Paul Celan wrote: "A poem . . . can be a message in a bottle, sent out in the—not always greatly hopeful—belief that somewhere and sometime it could wash up on land, on heartland perhaps" (Bremen Prize speech, trans. John Felstiner).

like the spear and shield
of seafaring men.
Whatever they beseech on my behalf,
these letters that go forth signed and sealed by my hand,
I will not ask for it openly   10
from the hand of flesh and blood
because of the disgrace
—as if I had no need of their strong hand
nor the gifts they grant.
And whatever does not leave this house   15
may wear out swiftly as a moth-eaten garment
with no one to serve
and preserve it, to confer on it
the palpable volume and value of a broken potsherd.
Here I stand, less than the least,   20
there's no point in wasting words about it,
composing epithets.
Whatever leaves here like a letter in a bottle
will go forth and pass through the waters,
will go forth, crossing the waters,   25
be tossed on the waves, swept along in the breakers,
and the glass may crack, the bottle
sink down in the sea.
Still, where there's a bottle tossed into the water,
there's hope   30
that the palm of a hand will grasp it, an eye will behold it,
a human being one day will say of it in wonder:
I found a bottle.

Lines 13–14, *as if I had no need of . . . the gifts*. Alluding to the Blessing after Meals, "May we never find ourselves in need of gifts or loans from flesh and blood, but may we rely only upon Your helping hand . . . ; thus we shall never suffer shame."

Line 16, *a moth-eaten garment*. Cf. Isa. 50:9, "They shall all wear out like a garment; the moth will devour them" (REB); Job 13:28.

He Crashed before Takeoff

His face is all he's got,
a countenance that won't reveal its features.
The head sunk between his shoulders,
sunk now in sleep.
His face is all he's got,   5
a scrim of confidence pulled over his face;
nothing shows through
but the gum line of his incisors.

As the tiger gnaws at the wild ox,
that's how doubt eats away at me.   10
What lops off my imaginings
is the sharp line between permitted and forbidden.

A passing breeze, a rap and a tap,
and if a single thought rises in my heart
it's as if I were touched by the tiger's paw.   15

The Story of the Arab Who Died in the Fire

When the fire seized his body, it didn't happen by slow degrees.
No burst of heat to begin with,
no stifling billow of smoke
no prospect of a room next door where one could escape.
The fire took him all at once,   5
such a thing hath not its likeness,
it peeled away his clothing
seized upon his flesh,

Title, *The Story of the Arab*. In a 1996 interview with the news daily *Yediot Acharonot*, Ravikovitch said: "As to the [poem about the Palestinian] day worker [from the Occupied Territories], when Jews nailed shut the door of the warehouse where he was sleeping, so he couldn't get out when it was set on fire—I wrote that poem because I understand the fear he felt before he was saved by death."

the first casualties were the nerves in the skin
then the hair fell prey to the fire, 10
God, they're burning us, he screamed,
that's all he could manage in self-defense.
The flesh was blazing along with the planks of the shed
that sustained the fire in the primary phase.
By that point his mental faculties were gone, 15
the firebrand of the flesh
paralyzed any sense of a future,
the memories of his family
the links to his childhood.
He was shrieking, no longer constrained by reason, 20
by now all the bonds of family were broken,
he did not seek vengeance, redemption, the dawn of a new day.
All he wanted was to stop burning
but his own body kept feeding the blaze
as if he were bound and laid on the altar 25
though he wasn't thinking about that, either.
He went on burning by the sheer force of his body,
flesh, fatty tissue and sinews.
And he kept on burning for a long time.
From his throat issued inhuman voices 30
since many human functions had already ceased
except for the pain transmitted in electrical pulses
along neural pathways to pain receptors in the brain.
All of this lasted no more than a single day.
And it's a good thing he breathed his last when he did 35
because he deserved to rest.

Line 10, *fell prey to the fire*, line 16, *firebrand* (Heb. *ma'akholet esh*). Isa. 9:5, 19, a rare biblical portmanteau combining the sense of "fuel of fire" with *ma'achelet*, a ritual slaughtering knife (Gen. 22:6). See "The Blue West."

Lullaby

Mama and Grandma
will sing you a song,
your shining white mothers
will sing you a song,
Mama's shawl brushes   5
your bed with its wing.
Mama and Grandma
a mournful old tune
will sing in Jabalya's cordon of gloom.
There they sat, clinging together as one: 10
Papa wrecked, coughing up
blood from his lung,
his son of fifteen embracing his frame
like a steel hoop girding
his father's crushed form   15
—what little remained.
True loves,
sweet doves,
thus did their captors make mock of them.

Mama and Grandma   20
will sing you a song
so you, sweet child,
may sleep without harm.

Title. *Lullaby.* An early version of the poem was published in July 1989 in the Israeli journal *Politika* under the title "A Lullaby Translated from the Yiddish." The text incorporated prose excerpts from the testimony of Israeli soldiers involved in the death by beating of a Palestinian man. The Yiddish lullaby has traditionally been a vehicle for expressions of national lament.

Line 8, *a mournful old tune* (Heb. *zemer atik ve-nugeh*). A pastiche of allusions to a Zionist folksong and popular poems by Rachel Bluvstein and Natan Alterman.

Line 9, *Jabalya.* Largest Palestinian refugee camp in the Gaza Strip, just north of Gaza City, a focal point of resistance to the Occupation.

Line 19, *captors.* Psalm 137:3, "For there they that carried us away captive required of us a song." See "The Captors Require a Song" and "What a Time She Had!"

Rachel is weeping aloud for her sons.
A lamentation. A keening of pain.   *25*
When thou art grown and become a man,
the grief of Jabalya thou shalt not forget
the torment of Shati thou shalt not forget,
Hawara and Beita,
Jelazoun, Balata,   *30*
their cry still rises night after night.

Free Associating

What does she have to say?
What does she have to say?
What else does she have to say?
She's got a perverted desire for suffering.
Well, in our country we have such lovely landscapes,   *5*
vineyards perched on the mountainside,
the shadow of clouds on the plain
and light
and a fenced-in plot of land;
and three rows of olive trees too,   *10*
uprooted as a punitive measure.
And three old women, their teeth rooted out.
Because of old age, of course, what else?
Violence isn't everything.
Why, of all things, on a bright clear Shabbat,   *15*
a perfectly happy Shabbat,

Lines 24–25, *Rachel . . . lamentation.* Jer. 31:15, "lamentation and bitter weeping;
Rachel, weeping for her children, refused to be comforted." See "But She Had a Son";
cf. "Like Rachel" and "Rough Draft." *A keening of pain* (Heb. *nekha'im,* a hapax), Isa.
16:7.

Line 27, *thou shalt not forget.* Deut. 25:17, 19, redirecting the command, "Remember
what Amalek did unto thee. . . . [T]hou shalt blot out the remembrance of Amalek
from under heaven; thou shalt not forget it." See "The Fruit of the Land."

Lines 28–30, *Shati.* Refugee camp in the Gaza Strip. *Hawara and Beita.* Villages near
Nablus in the West Bank. *Jelazoun.* Refugee camp near Ramallah in the West Bank.
Balata. Largest refugee camp in the West Bank, on the outskirts of Nablus.

Line 31, *their cry.* Cf. 1 Sam. 5:12, "the cry of the city went up to heaven."

does the memory of that man
have to sneak up again, the one they beat to death?
Ye shall not kill that man and his son both in one day.

The blot of a light cloud   20
has settled down over the plain.
In Zikhron Ya'akov, the vineyards are bursting
with the nectar of grapes.
Our storehouses are filled with grain
our wadis with water,   25
but turn over any stone
and out creeps a scorpion.
The Song of Nature.
And that Arab they beat to death.
Actually broke his body with their blows.   30
But not in Zikhron Ya'akov
and not in Mazkeret Batya,
those sleepy old towns of the Baron de Rothschild
that blend so nicely into the landscape.

What does she have to say?   35
What does she have to say?
She's just looking for ways to suffer,
to say a bad word.
She's not one of us,
she can't see what's good and beautiful in life.   40
She won't see us the way we are.
Anu banu artza:
We Came to Build the Land.

Line 19, *Ye shall not kill . . . both in one day*. Lev. 22:28, "And whether it be cow or
ewe, ye shall not kill it and its young both in one day."

Line 24, *Our storehouses are filled with grain*. A patriotic song from the 1950s, based
on Prov. 3:10, "So shall thy barns be filled with plenty, and thy presses shall burst out
with new wine."

Line 25, *wadi*. Riverbed that is dry except in the rainy season.

Line 29, *that Arab they beat*. See "Lullaby."

Lines 31, 32, *Zikhron Ya'akov, Mazkeret Batya*. Agricultural settlements in pre-State
Israel, established 1882 under the patronage of Baron Edmund de Rothschild, a phi-
lanthropist also instrumental in the founding of Israel's wine industry.

Line 42, *Anu banu artza*. The opening words of a well-known pre-State pioneer song,
"We came to the Land [to build it and be rebuilt in it]."

Rina Slavin

Rina Slavin lies abed all day,
pen and paper beside her
three cups with the dregs of coffee and tea,
a bottle of pills
and for added drama, two deodorants.   5
Opens her eyes with relish
all afire toward the new day,
but does not raise her body
from her lair.
Could it be she is paralyzed,   10
could it be she is lazy or—to use a higher style—
an idler?

A small alarm clock is at her bedside,
so should she wish to be alarmed into waking
there's nothing to prevent it.   15
Rina glances at the clock and discovers
half the morning is already gone.
And what will become of the other half?
What will come at noon
and yet again after noon   20
and just before eventide
with the splendiferous sunset so close to her window
that she, in any case, will miss.

Rina Slavin waves an enervated arm
to banish an ant or a hair   25
that sullies the sheet or the floor.
Her house is spotless, spick-and-span,
and the clock without ticking propels its hands
by her pillow or her bed.
No way will she ever manage   30
to cut and carve the times into hours
because she has no time

Line 12, *an idler*. Exod. 5:17, "Idlers, you are idlers!" (Alter, *Five Books of Moses*), from
Pharaoh's accusation of the Israelite slaves.

in the usual sense of the word.
She has a great wild hope
to arise, arise out of bed   35
and shake the world
or just
arise and shake her booty
like Deborah the Prophetess
and Miriam the sister of Moses,   40
but like Michal the wife of David
all she does is look out the window
despising in her heart.
All that despising, from within
and without, rends her asunder   45
and she defiles her days,
piping away
without so much as a flute to play.
Caught between the forces of nature that despoil her
she dozes off,   50
which is the best way of all
to swallow time,
swallow time.

Leafy Greenery

It is the year one thousand nine hundred and ninety
according to the Western reckoning.
An unruly greenery runs over with mercy, fills the window,
flecked with scattered flowers, pinkish yellow
like the bits of an omelet that fell apart.   5
No big red flower erupts from that green,

Line 35, *arise, arise,* and line 39, *like Deborah*. Judges 5:7, "I, Deborah arose, arose a mother in Israel."

Line 40, *Miriam*. Exod. 15:20, "And Miriam the prophetess . . . took a timbrel in her hand; and all the women went out after her with timbrels and with dances."

Line 41, *Michal*. 2 Sam. 6:16, 20: "Michal . . . looked out of a window, and saw King David leaping and dancing before the Lord; and she despised him in her heart."

a big flower is nowhere to be seen.
The year one thousand nine hundred and ninety
is not the year for big flowers.
In front of that greenery, a shutter with slats open wide,   10
and in front of the shutter, lace curtains
all flounces and furbelows.
That was the very worst year of my life.
And the green of the trees oozes pity
like Materna Infant Formula   15
(Ingredients: synthetic mother's milk, calcium and minerals).
My darling, a year of green shade and light,
a few yards of lacework and a shutter of gaping slats
do not amount to a year in the life.
In the year one thousand nine hundred and ninety   20
the life drained out of me
like those Dead of the Desert whose bodily fluids dried up
as they waited for rescue.

To Every Thing There Is a Season

Now the child has gone away,
he won't be home this Saturday.
And all the while, the palm tree grows.
The house crouches on all floors.
Without a sound, larvae of light   5
move in and out the shutter slat.
The shutter is locked, the bed's unmade.
My house is divided against itself,

Line 22, *Dead of the Desert*. Alluding to "The Last Dead of the Desert" (1897), an early allegorical poem by Bialik comparing European Jews to the biblical desert generation and exhorting them to abandon their passivity.

Title, *To Every Thing There Is a Season*. Eccl. 3:1.

Line 1, *the child has gone away*. Ravikovitch lost custody of her only son Ido in 1989; see "When the Eyes Open."

one half polished and well arrayed,
the other burnt black as a coal. 10
I'm cold and hot, hot and cold.
The child is gone for a hundred years,
a hundred years commence today.
He may come back for an hour or a day
but he won't stay. 15

When the Eyes Open

Snow on the mountains
above the high places
and above Jerusalem.
Come down O Jerusalem
and return my child to me. 5
Come O Bethlehem
and return my child to me.
Come high mountains
come winds
come floods in the harbors 10
and return my child to me.
And even you, O bent bulrush,
thin stalk in the stream,
stringy desert bushes,
return my child to me 15
as the soul returns to the body
when the eyes open.

Line 5, *return my child to me*. See "To Every Thing There Is a Season."

Line 12, *bent bulrush*. An allusion to Isaiah's critique of hypocritical piety (Isa. 58:5).

Lines 16–17, *as the soul returns . . . when the eyes open*. Echoes *Modeh Ani*, a prayer recited upon waking in the morning, thanking God for returning the soul to the body.

History of the Individual

for Yitzhak Livni

Nine words I said to you
You said this and that
You said: You've got a son
you've got time and you've got poetry.
The bars on the window were graven into my skin.   5
You won't believe I endured it.
I wasn't obliged
to bear it, really, as a human being, I mean.
On the tenth of Tevet was the siege laid
On the seventeenth of Tammuz was the city breached   10
On the ninth of Av was the Temple destroyed.
In all of this I was alone.

Line 9, *tenth of Tevet . . . siege.* Launching the Babylonian conquest of Jerusalem and destruction of the First Temple, 586 B.C.E. (2 Kings 25:1–4).

Line 10, *seventeenth of Tammuz.* According to rabbinic tradition, the date when Titus breached the walls of Jerusalem, leading to the destruction of the Second Temple (70 C.E.); here conflated with the destruction of the First Temple.

Line 11, *ninth of Av.* According to the Talmud (Mishnah *Ta'anit* 4:6), the date when both First and Second Temples were destroyed. *Temple* (Heb. *bayit,* lit. "house"). In biblical and rabbinic culture, a common metaphor for the female body.

Line 12, *I was alone.* Inverting the prophets' metaphor of city-as-woman; cf. Lam. 1:1, "How doth the city sit solitary, that was full of people; how is she become as a widow!" See "Sargeant Major Eyal Sameach."

The Captors Require a Song

How shall we sing of the songs of Zion
when we as yet hear not?
                        —Leah Goldberg

Sing us one of the songs of Zion
for an ear that hears not.
Sing us some insider songs
that the soul will recoil from singing
beyond the innermost circle   5
of the Home.
Quick, sing us a new song,
a song we will yank from your throat with pliers.
What are the Veil of the Ark and the Holy Temple
to you?   10
We've got a brute urge to inflict pain,
to torment.
For what are we without the cup of your sorrows?
A broken potsherd.
A broken potsherd too the loathing in your throat.   15

Epigraph, *Leah Goldberg*. A slightly altered quote from Goldberg's 1959 poem, "From the Songs of Zion." See "The Bullfrogs."

Title and line 1, *Sing . . . the songs of Zion*. Cf. Psalm 137:3, "For there they that carried us away captive required of us a song; and they that wasted us required of us mirth, saying, Sing us one of the songs of Zion." See "What a Time She Had!" and "Lullaby."

Line 2, *an ear that hears not*. Cf. Isa. 6:9–10, "Make the mind of this people dull, and stop their ears, and shut their eyes, so that they may not look with their eyes, and listen with their ears and comprehend with their minds, and turn and be healed" (NRSV).

Line 6, *Home* (Heb. *bayit*). A polyvalent term whose meaning includes house, home, the national homeland, and the Temple. See "History of the Individual."

Line 7, *a new song*. Psalm 33:3.

Line 9, *Veil of the Ark* (Heb. *parokhet*). See Exod. 26:33, "and the veil shall divide unto you between the holy place and the most holy."

Look at us:
We hung your harps
far, far away
upon the willows.
And you: Keep on sawing   20
with your cracked voices
like a donkey climbing
the Ladder of Tyre
or a lowing ox
buzz buzz.   25

Line 17, *We hung your harps*. Cf. Psalm 137:2, "We hanged our harps upon the willows in the midst thereof."

Lines 22, 24, *donkey, ox*. Associated with the coming of the Messiah.

Line 23, *Ladder of Tyre*. A narrow passage, historically a series of steps cut into the rock, between the mountains and the sea, on the route taken by the Israeli forces in the 1982 invasion of Lebanon.

New

Poems

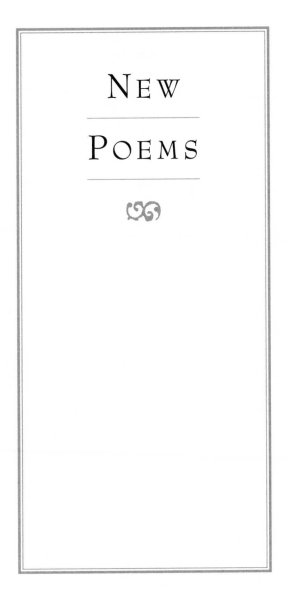

There Is No Fear of God in This Place

"Surely there is no love in this place, nor will there ever be,"
Father would tell me
from his picture hanging on the wall year after year,
"and human mercy is like a barleycorn
that teeth gnaw upon,"   5
so Father would tell me.
"When I was run over and killed on that black road,
in an eyeblink, alone,
struck to the ground, startled and shamed,
in that eyeblink I knew: 10
In all the years to come
like me you'd remain startled,
you wouldn't beware of fire
nor of ocean torrents;
like me, you would have no hand   15
to wrest you away from danger.
Fifty years and more I'd be gazing at you from that picture
and all of a sudden we'd burst out laughing
for no apparent reason.
Surely there is no love in this place   20
except for the love between two.
And whoever tore you from me—
there was no fear of God in his heart,
nor will there ever be."

Title, *There Is No Fear of God in This Place*. Gen. 20:11, Abraham's mistrust of the
moral character of Abimelech's people. The phrase "fear of God" is used in biblical
Hebrew in situations involving ethical conduct.

Line 7, *When I was run over*. See Ravikovitch's early poem on her father's untimely
death, "On the road at night there stands the man."

Lines 17–21, *Fifty years . . . the love between two*. The Hebrew lines are inscribed on
Ravikovitch's tombstone.

Conversation with a Photo

Why don't you even try, man?
Leaning against the wall, you can see
yet you keep your mouth shut.
In a conservative shirt, your head erect.
Your eyes give off a guarded sensitivity.   5
But the face isn't life size;
visible indications of the touch-up pencil
in the shadows between chin and neck.
What willpower I invest to grant you
years of virtual existence.   10
And you want and you don't want
and you pass yourself off as a man who can see
and you do not do, you do not do
anymore
what a beloved father would do.   15

Oxygen

A tiny lizard on the wall of your house, Ido,
that's what I want to be.
One frond of the fern in the planter,
a sheet of paper, a tablecloth, an ashtray,
a current events notebook, a drawing.   5
All these are your daily companions,
they see you and are absorbed
into your field of vision.
No need to look for an emotional response.
I just want to be in your physical vicinity,   10
set down, unseen.
With no purpose,
enclosed in a space
where you inhale, exhale, inhale, exhale
oxygen.   15
We're not talking about love, Ido.

I want to be the whitewash on the wall,
the window lintel, the sock drawer
in the room that soaks up the process
of your metabolism
eight hours every night.

20

The Way of All Nature

A human being goes out of his house
in the morning or at noon
or in the evening
and he's gone.
What does it mean, gone? 5
After all, whoever is not here
is there.
But the plain sense of gone is *whirled away*,
i.e., he deserts; i.e., is deserted;
i.e., gone with the wind. 10
And the interpretation according to
the way of all nature:
darkness upon the face of the deep.
Hence the name of that place is called *world*
as in *whirled away*. 15

Memento

When my little boy got all tuckered out
climbing that steep hill in San Francisco,

Line 8, *plain sense . . . is* (Heb. *ki-fshuto . . . perusho*). Mimicking the Talmudic
method of literal interpretation (*pshat*).

Line 13, *darkness upon the face of the deep.* Gen. 1:2.

Line 14, *Hence the name of that place is called.* Mimicking the biblical method of
explaining place names.

I was huffing and puffing like him.
I didn't know how we'd manage to ascend
all the way to the mountaintop and the threshold of home.   5
Ten years ago.
Even a difficult evening will turn into night,
into morning again. The crooked shall be made plain.
Not so San Francisco.

She won't deign to stoop from her heights, not even a bit,   10
not for pity or terror.
Her senses swept by her self-loving beauty and her mighty winds
wafting the scent of marijuana
—that's what takes her mind off the earthquakes.
Terror and grandeur are the source of her nonchalance.   15
Her beauty plunged into me like a knife
dipped in the fume of poppies.

I too left her a memento:
With a tiny secret stream,
small and rounded as a buttonhole,   20
I made my mark close to shore.
And the raging waters of the bay paid it no heed,
so wee it was.

The Hope of the Poet

What's up with you,
O young poets,
that you write so much about poetry
and the art of the poem
and the use of materials,   5

Line 5, *mountaintop . . . threshold of home.* Mock-messianic, cf. Isa. 2:2, Ezek. 10:4.
Line 8, *crooked . . . plain.* Isa. 40:4; title of a well-known 1912 novella by S. Y.
Agnon.

God forbid
writer's block
should descend upon you
and wreak havoc.

For lo, a remedy is at hand   10
to banish all grief:
to repose at the breakfast table
with its slightly faded oilcloth,
mooning at the windowpane
till the noon hour draws nigh.   15
And should slumber seize you, banish it not,
nor set at naught the taste of honey and butter.
Thou shalt not multiply poems and poesies,
nay, thou shalt do no work at all,
and should thy heart find ease,   20
conceal it for many days
lest any eye behold.
For why dost thou make haste, my dear,
to take the slippery poem by the horns
or goad it between the ribs   25
the way a lone Bedouin lad shall lead
his tarrying ass?

After all, any good that may come of this
in the best of all possible worlds,
even after appeals to the mayor's office,   30
is a grave dug just for you

Line 7, *writer's block* (Heb. *shtikat ha-meshorer*). An allusion to Bialik's long poetic silence after he emigrated to Palestine from Odessa.

Line 19, *thou shalt do no work*. An ironic reference to the commandment to do no work on the Sabbath, Exod. 20:10, Deut. 5:14.

Lines 25–27, *goad . . . tarrying ass*. A pastiche of apocalyptic references. The Messiah is supposed to arrive "lowly, and riding upon an ass," Zech. 9:9; it is forbidden to "goad the footsteps of the Messiah," i.e., to hasten the End of Days, cf. Hab. 2:3: "though it tarry, wait for it"; the well-known hymn *Ani Ma'amin* ("I Do Believe") affirms a faith in the coming of the Messiah "though he tarry." Cf. Isa. 11:6, "a little child shall lead them."

in the Writers' Section
of the cemetery on Trumpeldor Street,
a sixty-meter dash
from Bialik's Tomb. 35

Line 33, *cemetery on Trumpeldor Street.* Where the leaders and writers of the early Hebrew Yishuv are buried; established 1902 and closed many years ago. No amount of effort could now get any poet buried in that cemetery; indeed, Ravikovitch herself is buried in the Kiryat Shaul cemetery.

Line 35, *Bialik.* See "The Bullfrogs," "The Law of Gravitation," "Leafy Greenery," and "Child Boy Man."

MANY

WATERS

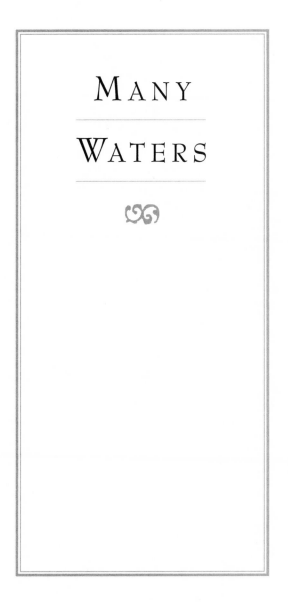

Many Waters

A ship
afloat with no anchor.
She does have a sail
but the sea has no wind.
The sea expands,   5
spills into the ocean.
All across the horizon
no shade.
The ship's an antique
from the fourteen hundreds.   10
No motor on board.
For the Indies she sails.
The bread grows stale.
A plague erupts inside her.
The sail is torn.   15
Fresh water's gone.
Maybe a native canoe will come
bearing maize
or something to chew on.
The captain despairs.   20
Jumps into the waters.
He'd rather drown.
Meanwhile he floats
not far from the ship.
Through the spyglass   25
the second mate sees
no Indies, no bread,
no meat and no fish.
A sailor gnaws on a rotten plank.
The hunger's horrific.   30
The ship will get nowhere.
She's gone astray.
This ship

Title, *Many Waters*. Cf. Psalm 18:16, "he drew me out of many waters," and Song of
Songs 8:7, "Many waters cannot quench love, neither can the floods drown it."

is the *Dahlia Maria*.
She will sink today, 35
she is sinking today.

As Though I Were Not

Don't do that to me,
I'm not of such little account
that you should blot me out
as though I were not.
Between us we had something 5
quick and lovely,
between us we had
flickerings
like two ship lanterns shining
on one another. 10
Not the same night
and not the same sea.

And whatever we wrecked
was just the way of all flesh and blood.
I am a ship 15
and you are a ship,
better armored, perhaps.
How can you and I navigate
such unquiet waters.
Hide not thyself, do not blot me out, 20
and do not behave
as though I were not,
for whatever you do unto me

Line 36, *sinking*. See "The Roar of the Waters," "Growing Poor," and "A Far-Reaching Athletic Exercise."

Line 20, *Hide not thyself*. Cf. Psalm 10:1, "Why hidest thou thyself in times of trouble?" and the sixteenth-century liturgical poem, familiar as a Sabbath hymn, *Eleh chamda libi* ("This is the desire of my heart; please have pity and hide not thyself").

will turn back on you,
and often I too appear to myself   25
as though I were not.

Guilt Feelings

Guilt feelings, I've got them in spades
but not the way you imagine.
On Yom Kippur I don't fast
but I don't go looking for thrills either
because hunger isn't conducive to personality enhancement,   5
it won't purify, only irritate,
and I know from experience
and from study and observation
how to be irritating to others as well as myself.
I'm still evolving, becoming more efficient,   10
since overcoming the simplest obstacle
is an unattainable goal.
And this whole business drags on and on, like the hamsins
on an army outpost, on the highway or in the loony bin,
drags on like feast days and holidays   15
with no schedule no family
no attention span,
and it's a good thing I've got my zip code down pat
so the mail can be delivered, as long as
nobody sends me a package   20
too big for the mailbox
since one thing I won't do is go to the post office
out of laziness and impatience
and lack of motivation, to boot.
And this confession, written in a vacuum,   25
and in order to avoid cooking and cleaning

Lines 13–14, *the hamsins on an army outpost* (Heb. *Hamsinim ba-mishlat*). The title of
a popular blues song from the early 1960s about the existential ennui of soldiers on an
outpost, sung by the Nachal Army Band. A hamsin is a hot dry desert wind.

and doing the laundry,
is a story that has no end
and won't have one either
till winter rolls around   30
or a donkey climbs up the ladder,
whichever comes first.

Three or Four Cyclamen

Three or four white cyclamen
and I have one more plant with leaves aplenty
that keeps ascending to the ceiling,
and I have troves of treasure hidden away
and I have a little secret, nothing shocking,   5
that seeps down into the vein in my palm
and colors my blood a lustrous red.
You're busy now, so many accounts to settle,
you're not thinking about me, not talking,
up there in your exalted heights,   10
hovering
like a delicate mist that consorts with the clouds
and besprinkles them with the pearly dust of dawn.
I always knew you would treat me this way.
This is just a trifling story   15
with no hidden meaning.
But that mountain descending into the sea
straight down to translucent turquoise waters
has forgotten you.
That mountain is mine, all mine,   20
not yours.

Line 31, *donkey.* Associated with the coming of the Messiah; see "The Captors Require
a Song" and "The Hope of the Poet." Here a mock-apocalyptic reference.

Kite in an Empty Sky

He's not a full-fledged bird but a lot like one
up there in the sky for my eyes to see.
What a beak he's got, one imitation wing
and a body to behold,
straight nose, broad prow.   5
He's a very light weight, belly and stern,
doesn't freeze in the wind
in the sun he won't burn,
he's not mine at all
but only in my eyes   10
does he amount to anything
for no one knows better than me
what it is that flies
and does not fall
and will not bruise.   15
Now on Shabbat
at noon
in Metula by chance
with no intimation of danger
I see him   20
and he doesn't even see the sharp knife,
the whetted knife
that could wound me, not him
since I'm down here on earth
and he's up there in the sky.   25
So what do I care,
what does he care.
We're unlike as unlike can be, it's true,
as unlikely a pair as any two.

Line 18, *Metula*. A small town on the Israel-Lebanon border.

Lines 28, 29, *unlike, unlikely*. The Hebrew pun here links "being different" (*shonim*)
with "being two" (*shnayim*).

Child Boy Man

What will become of you in the end, my child,
and what will become of me?
For seven years we lived at the mouth of a volcano
in a cloud of sulphurous fumes.
Run, run for your life, my child,   5
climb on the wings of seagulls.
It's your mother (that's me) telling you this:
Sheep and oxen nibble the grass
but the fiery sons of Reshef soar
as the sparks fly upward.   10
Only one songbird is missing there
without wings without a beak.
That's my bird, I mean, more like me than any other.
Mother and child, child and mother
—a story that never ends. And then   15
in a flash
children grow up and turn into men.

Etc. Etc.

What is love? I asked Ido
and he cast me a sidelong glance
and told me pouting or in pity:
If you don't know by now

Line 3, *at the mouth of a volcano*. A common Israeli expression for living in a volatile political situation.

Line 8, *oxen . . . grass*. Cf. Num. 22:4.

Lines 9–10, *Reshef . . . upward*. An ancient Near Eastern god of fire and lightning. The phrase *bney reshef* (lit. "sons of Reshef") in Job 5:7 is usually translated "sparks"; rabbinic sources take it to mean mythical flying creatures.

Line 11, *songbird* (Heb. *tzipor shir*). Also "bird of poetry," i.e., the Muse. The Shekhina, the feminine presence of God, is often described as a bird. An allusion to Bialik's first published poem, "To the Bird."

Line 12, *without wings without a beak*. See "Hide and Seek."

you won't ever know.   5
Then I told him without pity or pout
but with a winsome side-glance, a bit bemused,
I do know what love is,
all I wanted was to test your way with words
and your proficiency in Hebrew   10
and I also wanted a drop of pity and anger
to maintain the suspense,
so we won't start boring one another
and get into fighting and apologizing,
that kind of thing just eats me up.   15
I do know what love is.
For example: I love you.

More on the Matter of Ido

I'm reading nice and slow these days,
I focus with attentive gaze
and suddenly it all seems open wide.

I'll be seeing you anon,
you lizard tail that's here and gone   5
the way it came, an arrow speeding up.

What I want is not a lot,
just Ido back here each Shabbat
and white puff pastry from the baker's shop.

What I want is just to stay   10
alone at night. Right here, I say,
there's nothing bad that I cannot abide.

And Ido still is my mainstay,
whether near or far away.
So glad that you're already at my side,   15

a grown-up son yet somehow still a pup.

Half an Hour before the Monsoon

Half an hour before the monsoon
the ox pulling the cart didn't flare its nostrils
and I myself hoisted my boy up
and told him I had hopes of him
but meanwhile he needs to buckle down   5
like the rest of us
and get the animal its feed,
and my wife and my mother worked together in the kitchen
and I was thinking about a small business
making batik or souvenirs   10
for the tourists. And the little one, she cut her finger
on a bit of iron in the yard
and the air was hot and motionless
and my clothes so drenched with sweat they stuck to me,
and all of a sudden clouds gathered and the monsoon came   15
and the little one, she was swept away in the murky
current of mud, and that suffocation
was the worst torture,
and my son was saved maybe, maybe not
but he's quick on his feet   20
and besides he wasn't with us just then.
I had hopes of him.

In the Year to Come, in the Days to Come

My mother lies in bed now, trying to die.
Eight years have passed, morning like evening
evening like morning,
and the hours seconds minutes between—
empty   5
lean.
My mother paid no heed
to flowers and all that blooming nonsense,
lightning storms, the beauty of nature.
Eight years and not one moment left her   10

any the wiser, pulled her to her feet
nor restored her will power,
the Joy of Work, the ability to remember
something so vital to her being
as the Ethical Teachings of the Jews.   *15*

My mother lies in bed now, trying to die.
All of a sudden she rears up like a lioness
in protest, and says without words: I've had my fill,
I've had it with living.
In the days to come   *20*
in the year to come
all the glorious flowers of the Galilee
will just have to bloom without me.

She Doesn't Really Know

Words (what words?) can kill,
what do you mean, "kill"?
Words are so pure, so skilled,
they can cross the road
bridge what's apart   *5*
let you pour out your heart.
If something explodes,
take my hand, dear,
let's get out of here.

No supper for you   *10*
said Roni Simchoni to the little girl, age seven,
'cause you didn't do your job today.
Then she let her off
and let her eat
the same grubby gruel as usual.   *15*

*   *   *

Line 11, *Roni Simchoni.* An ironic literalization of a common Hebrew name: Roni (root *r.o.n.*, "sing with joy"), Simchoni (root *s.m.ch.*, "be happy").

Roni died of cancer before her time.
Any connection to the above
is purely coincidental.
Decades passed without wisdom or peace.
To Michal they said: We'll make you wide doors 20
in your home that is not your home
since you are a passing phenomenon.
Whoever's next in this room
may need a wheelchair, a swinging door,
a shower seat. 25
This is your home, but just for a while.
Settle down, sleep and eat,
feel free to walk anywhere you like,
Freedom Is Our Finest Feature.
After all, don't you know, 30
a person your age is a terminal creature.

And my mother, Michal,
met all those expectations
and then some.
In the wheelchair she sat, 35
staring off into space.
Seven years in that place
from bed to chair,
eating the light bill of fare.
Only once in a while would she say: 40
This is not my home,
not this one, for sure.
Words (what words?) can't kill.
Especially words of reasoned knowledge
that put the mind at rest. 45
And now my mother enjoys perfect rest
though without perfect joy
since she doesn't really know.

The Feast of Love without Mama

On the eve of Tu be-Av the moon grew full
in memory of my mother
who died in the spring on some date or other
in some year or other
and I told her: *Mazal tov,*   5
Mama. *Mazal tov,* you managed to die
because what you had was no life,
just humiliation and chill all about you.
And I was pleased for you
that you set out on such a joyful journey   10
on a moonbeam,
and ditched that gray sweatsuit
and the people who never came to visit
and the TV that was always tuned
to Channel Two.   15
You had a lot of *mazal,* Mama,
which does not contradict the fact
that your absence is hard for me,
especially now on the eve of the Feast of Love.
You had no feast and you had no love,   20
only a long-drawn-out Tish'a be-Av
that lasted eight years.
Though you loved life more than I do,
you knew how to put an end to it
with the obstinacy of a peasant eaten by quiet anger.   25

Mama, are you still angry?

Title, *The Feast of Love,* and line 1, *Tu be-Av.* The Fifteenth of Av, which usually
falls in July/August, the Israeli Valentine's Day; originally a matchmaking day for
unmarried women in the Second Temple period. Like some other Jewish holidays,
it is celebrated in the middle of the month of the Hebrew lunar calendar, when the
moon is full.

Line 5, *Mazal tov.* Congratulations; lit. "good fortune."

Line 15, *Channel Two.* The popular commercial television channel.

Line 21, *Tish'a be-Av.* The Ninth of Av, a day of fasting, commemorating the destruc-
tion of the First and Second Temples.

Rectangular Picture in an Oval Frame

Mosya, my boy-uncle,
you must know I wouldn't boast before you
nor act holier-than-thou.
I'm ill at ease with you
and it's more than I can bear,   5
keeping you alive all by myself, seventy-eight years
after your death.
You are a picture hanging in an oval frame.
The frame maker had quite a time
fitting it around the retouched rectangular photo.   10
And now you are hanging in a prominent place
in my room.
On purpose, so I'll be asked: Who's that?
And many do ask: Is that your father?
And I give a practiced smart-aleck answer,   15
not at all spontaneous:
Why on earth my father?
He's hardly even my uncle.
Which is to say: You died, struck down at a time when I
hadn't yet appeared in your mind's eye.   20
Maybe you'd have been too selfish (I'd rather say: touchy)
to take note of me even if you'd lived a long time
and had truly become my uncle, my love.
I think that only my father, two years your junior, loved you.
The rest found you an arrogant braggart   25
but do the rest matter?
I'd rather have formed my own opinion
if you had only waited,
if you had managed to control the impulse
to self-destruct because of an aching mind.   30
Had you waited another fifteen years
you might have been steeled by my love,
the love of a baby girl

Line 1, *Mosya.* Affectionate nickname for Moshe among Russian-born Jews.

Line 23, *my uncle, my love* (Heb. *dodi ve-re'i*). Song of Songs 5:16; *dodi*, usually translated "my love," can also mean "my uncle."

who grew and matured to a ripe old age
and still remembers you with loving-kindness   35
and tells who you are and what you were,
and most of all thinks that a man like you, at whatever age,
is a heartbreaker of a man.
Mosya, my uncle, nineteen, when he died heartbroken.

Banalia

During the war on day twenty-two
I looked round and round at the hullabaloo.
The instincts of eating, aggression and sex
were just as they'd been,
who would've guessed?   5
Bored, we'd already climbed all the walls;
the sealed room concealed no treasure at all.
And the human pain flows
flows without cease
before the war and before the peace.   10

A Northern Winter's Day

How time flies.
I didn't hear you groan
didn't see you sit on your haunches
like an Arab,
a man in a Mt. Hermon parka with helmet and socks   5

Line 7, *sealed room*. During the 1990 Gulf War, Israelis were instructed to stay in a sealed room in their homes—now part of the required building code—wearing gas masks because of the fear that the Scuds launched by Iraq would carry chemical warheads.

Line 5, *Mt. Hermon*. Snow-capped ridge on the Lebanon-Syria border, partly occupied by Israel in 1967 and policed jointly by the Israeli army and the South Lebanon Army (SLA). *Mt. Hermon parka*. Standard IDF issue to soldiers serving in colder regions.

who doesn't really know Hebrew yet
but shares a cigarette with the SLA
salutes the company commander
and rides off on leave in an armored car
a solitary soldier,   10
then returns
pulls up the elastic band on his socks
and is hit at eleven o'clock in the morning
three and a half minutes before the cease-fire
or a massive artillery barrage   15
whatever comes first,
by whatever flies out of the barrel of a gun
of someone following an order or his heart's desire.
And someone or other, whatever his name may be,
took leave of his life at eleven o'clock in the morning   20
not intending to meet up with it again
in any of the possible worlds.
At the General Staff, there was general frustration
and they scrambled some planes or they didn't.
And there was great self-sacrifice   25
on one side or the other.

Three or four mothers were stricken with breast cancer
and at least one mother went into shock
at eleven in the morning.

In Metula they prepared trays of shish kebab skewers   30
and Arab salad for the field reporters who were on their way.
At eleven o'clock in the morning
someone quite frontline took leave of his life
ate no lunch, ate no supper
wrote no letters, made no calls.   35
Dead as the dead.

Line 13, *at eleven o'clock in the morning*. Echoing "at five in the afternoon" in Lorca's
"Lament for Ignacio Sánchez Mejías."

Line 30, *Metula*. See "Kite in an Empty Sky."

Briefing on the State of Affairs:
Beginning of Summer

At the produce stall they've got a ten-year-old working,
not one of our kids, God forbid
—one of theirs, the Arabs,
may their memory be wiped out for good.
They wanna throw us into the sea,   5
fat chance that's ever gonna be,
may God's mercy fall
on us and them all.
No love lost in this land
except among the young   10
who save up their measly shekels
to move to the States, making sure
to pack the CDs of the top singers
especially the ten in the starting lineup,
but the Jerusalem Beitar soccer team   15
boosts our morale
whenever they win,
but when Beitar loses
a national day of mourning is declared
in Jerusalem, City of David,   20
and only the Ultra-Orthodox
rejoice in the open and on the sly
and even spit on the monuments
to our beloved dead.
And you can't do a damn thing about it,   25
don't even try,
better shut your mouth
and who's got the strength to laugh or to cry,
the heroes are all worn out, all of them,
wiped out as the carcass of an ass from Shechem.   30

Line 15, *Beitar.* A wildly popular soccer team with a core of nationalist fans. The team
is affiliated with the right-wing youth movement by that name.

Line 30, *an ass* (Heb. *chamor*). Cf. also Hamor, father of Shechem, Gen. 34. *Shechem.*
An Israelite city associated with the patriarchs; modern-day Nablus in the occupied
West Bank.

Upside Down and Inside Out

Purim 1996
Bomb explosion on the No. 5 bus line

Heart of freedom, heart of light
Who was dark and who was slight
Who drummed on the drummer girl
hurled her up and made her whirl
Who told us plainly: *Blah blah bleep*   5
Rouse ye from your slumber deep
On Dizengoff Square at every light
you can't go straight, you can't turn right,
and turning left? Not in this town,
the whole shebang is inside out   10
—this Purimfest we won't beat Haman down.

Lines 1–2, *Heart of freedom, heart of light . . . dark.* Alludes to a short story by Amalia Kahana-Carmon, "Heart of Summer, Heart of Light," which in turn invokes Conrad's *Heart of Darkness.*

Line 3, *drummer girl.* Alludes to *The Little Drummer Girl* (1983), a spy novel by John le Carré dealing with the Palestinian armed resistance.

Line 7, *Dizengoff Square.* At the time, still the hub of Tel Aviv, named for its first mayor; the No. 5 bus line runs down this street. The poem conflates two suicide bombings, on the No. 5 bus on Dizengoff Street (Oct. 19, 1994) and outside the Dizengoff Center shopping mall (March 4, 1996).

Line 11, *Purim.* A carnivalesque holiday celebrating the deliverance of the Persian Jews from Haman, as told in the Book of Esther. The normative rules of conduct are turned upside down, and there are costume parades in the main streets of most towns.

Adloyada in Manhattan

By the rivers of Babylon, there we sat,
yea, on All Saints' Day
(in Manhattan)
and talked about Big Bucks
and fucks,   5
and about the awesome times
we had in the reserves
and the naval commando disaster
for which as usual there was no one to blame
except human error   10
like the Turkish plane
that took off and went down
(in the Bermuda Triangle)
'cause what's the diff?

And we talked at the top of our lungs   15
the way they holler on the balcony
in Tel Aviv or Tel Aviv-Jaffa,
Arabs and Jews,
and the Arabs wanted to throw us into the sea
as usual   20
and we took away their land
as usual,
and the general of some crack unit
rounded up a bunch of their minors
and gave it to them with a firehose, a wet maneuver,   25

Title, *Adloyada*. Purim parade and carnival. The name invokes the Talmudic directive, "A person should drink on Purim until he cannot distinguish [Heb. *ad lo yada*] between 'Cursed be Haman!' and 'Blessed be Mordecai!'" (Tractate *Megillah*).

Lines 1, 28, *By the rivers of Babylon, . . . yea, we wept.* Psalm 137:1. See "You Can't Kill a Baby Twice."

Line 8, *naval commando disaster.* An Israeli naval commando unit was caught in an ambush off the coast of Lebanon in September 1997, resulting in heavy casualties.

Line 17, *Jaffa.* A primarily Palestinian city, adjacent to Tel Aviv and predating it; Tel Aviv-Jaffa is a joint municipality.

'cause that's how they like it
they're used to it,
and yea, we wept when we remembered
the girls we met in the reserves
how we pumped their heads full of dirty jokes,   30
and our longings filled the land
and we didn't remember so good how to speak Hebrew,
'cause now what talks when we open our mouths
is money
and longing for the first night   35
as orphans without Mama and Papa.
'Cause what are we without Holon and Bat Yam
where Mama cooks squash
in hot sauce with *hilbeh*.
And the heart grows full.   40
And the heart beats fast.
And pounds at the temples.
First night without Mama
with a real hot number from Bat Yam
who scarfs down like a pig   45
what we left on the plate,
and this time there was no terror attack
on Halloween
thanks to the Colombian underground
that pumps us all full of heroween.   50

Line 37, *Holon . . . Bat Yam*. Lower- and middle-class towns south of Tel Aviv, which have a large concentration of immigrants and Middle Eastern Jews.

Line 39, *hilbeh*. A Middle Eastern condiment made from fenugreek.

Line 43, *First night without Mama*. The title of an Israeli song about a homesick soldier's first experiences in boot camp.

Line 47, *terror attack*. Purim, the Israeli Halloween, has been a time of terror alerts since the 1996 suicide bombing; see "Upside Down and Inside Out."

Swimming Practice

No ordinary man:
penniless, panhandling,
tongue-lashing,
backbiting,
badmouthing, befouling   5
in the current fashion.
Ripping off minds,
ripping off petty cash
from the poor box
because life trumps all.   10
Making a buck and living it up
—that's what reality demands.
An orphan
can kick very nicely
even in a riptide.   15
If you've got no God
and orphanhood is your métier,
you'd better know how to swim.

An Unsatisfactory Answer to the Question

What are your thoughts about the assassination of the Prime Minister?
Yes, what are your thoughts about the assassination
of the Prime Minister?
And what are your feelings?
Are you in a state of shock   5
or depression?
One might very well ask.

Lines 4–5, *backbiting . . . befouling*. A pastiche of biblical allusions condemning slander and corruption. Cf. Prov. 13:3, 20:19, Jer. 6:28, 9:3, Ezek. 22:9.

Line 1, *assassination*. Yitzhak Rabin was assassinated by a right-wing fanatic at a peace rally in Tel Aviv on November 4, 1995.

And do you have a stutter
or do you just not know where all this is headed,
do you sound so dazed   *10*
because of the future or the present,
one might very well ask.
Or is it perhaps that you feel like an idiot,
or are you not in your right mind?
Come on, answer.   *15*
And I answer:
Everything you have said is true
and you are a dear man.
And I wish to add one more thing, if I can.
The Prime Minister died a happy man.   *20*

Farewell to the dust of my Prime Minister,
husband and father, and what's rarely said:
son of Rosa the Red.

Sergeant Major Eyal Sameach

Sgt. Maj. Eyal Sameach,
whose name means Joyful Stag,
is no longer joyful
and not really sad
now that he's immersed   *5*
in eternal rest.
And I don't have one single word
of consolation
for the mother of Eyal Sameach
nor for his father   *10*
who will never again know joy.

Line 23, *Rosa the Red*. Nickname of Rabin's mother, a socialist activist in the His-
tadrut, the Israeli federation of labor unions; also the nickname of Rosa Luxemburg,
a heroic figure for Socialist Zionists early on.

How are the mighty fallen,
and we—how do we dispatch
you, eager children,
to a land of evil decree?   *15*
Children with a beret
of the Golani Brigade
or some other unit,
an elite unit, no doubt,
no man hath seen its like.   *20*
And what else can one say
to the mother of Eyal Sameach?
How doth the city sit solitary
that once was a multitude.

                    October 1995

Marina Haddad

Marina Haddad
lay alone on the bed,
on her eyes a wreath,
cinnamon on her mouth.
The field reporters and the TV corps   *5*
walked in the wrong door

Line 12, *How are the mighty fallen.* 2 Sam. 1:19, from King David's lament for Saul and
Jonathan, who died in battle. See "Attributes of the Human."

Line 15, *land of evil decree.* Lev. 16:22, "And the [scape]goat shall bear upon it all their
iniquities unto a land not inhabited" (Heb. *eretz gzera*). In modern Hebrew, *eretz gzera*
means a desolate region to which one is banished.

Line 17, *Golani.* A frontline infantry brigade in the Israeli army, often deployed in the
West Bank and Lebanon.

Lines 23–24, *How doth the city . . . multitude.* Opening words of the Book of Lamen-
tations. See "History of the Individual."

Title, *Marina Haddad.* Here a Christian Palestinian name.

and that was her only bit of luck
that night.
All the makings were there: bereavement, sorrow,
the mother a single parent,   10
the state of the nation as metonymy
for the fate of the individual (especially vice versa),
and no one could say for sure
if they got a sound bite of crying or not,
and Marina Haddad was quite calm   15
since the initial stage of death has its serenity.
She was one of a kind,
call it the luck of a goy that she alone
was not exploited
to diagnose the state of the nation   20
and forecast the inescapable ramifications.
Thus she lay nice and quiet
with a wreath or without
—sometimes a sheet can be an entire world.
And her mother, the single parent,   25
got there at four or five o'clock,
and what she endured
I'm at a loss to express
or even to fathom.
It's best not to pry into a matter   30
that cannot be fathomed.
Heartrending suffering is suffering that rends
the heart of the sufferer
alone.
Marina Haddad lay alone on the bed,   35
and you could say she was one lucky girl
at least for that hour, that hour and a half.
And as to what transpired next
I have no desire to tell.

The Poetics of Applying
"Moderate Physical Pressure"

dedicated to those who labor in the cause

Not to take any of it by force
one should never take anything by force.
One must always come carefully from behind
quickly cover the eyes of the man
and ask: Don't you recognize my voice?   5
How can it be you don't know my name?
Surely you must be jesting now,
what a subtle sense of humor you have
(the sweat begins to bead on his brow).
You're the father of my daughter, isn't that so?   10
She just turned seven years old this spring
(here I begin to tread on his toes).
Perhaps by now you've recalled my name
(with a blade to the nape, I part his skin).
The man cries and falls on all fours   15
but I don't release my hold on his eyes.
With his eyes blinded, he's got to guess
my name and learn of his daughter's birth
that I just made up as I opened my mouth.
The man writhes in the dust and cries,   20
blood runs down his neck, his eyes are inflamed.
Genteel as I am, and oh so well-bred,
I do not injure his testicles.
His mouth contorts in the effort to guess
my name in a flash of illumination.   25
Sigalit, he tells me in a phony voice,
I have never forgotten you, Sigalit.
Now's when I bash his head to the ground;

Title, *"Moderate Physical Pressure"* (Heb. *lachatz fizi matun*). The language of the Israeli Supreme Court, establishing what is permissible in interrogating Palestinian detainees. The expression is generally used as a euphemism for "torture."

there's no doubt the man deliberately lies,
his only wish is to save his own skin.   30
With a builder's spike I'll chisel on his skin:
"Keep thee ever far from a lie."
Then I'll lay him down on the sand to bleed;
by now my rage exceeds every bound.
How debased and despised was that man in my eyes   35
when he kept trying to guess my name.
But I did not take anything by force
one should never take anything by force.

Metamorphosis

The cat had a fit. Lashed himself with his tail.
First he raked his left paw with his right,
then stuck out a claw and thrust it in his eye;
the other eye he ploughed in parallel lines.

When he was drenched in blood, the cat felt best.   5
He shredded the flesh of his own right thigh,
yanked the left one out as a matter of course.
Soon his body turned into a muddy red mess.

By no means was he an irrational cat.
He slaughtered himself and suffered no pain,   10
for he'd longed all his life to become a dog,
sheepdog or wolfdog, it was all the same.

Line 32, *Keep thee ever far.* Exod. 23:7.

The Fruit of the Land

a farewell song to the good old days

You asked if we've got enough cannons
They laughed and said: More than enough
and we've got new improved antitank missiles
and bunker busters to penetrate
double-slab reinforced concrete   5
and we've got crates of napalm and crates of explosives,
unlimited quantities, cornucopias,
a feast for the soul, like some finely seasoned delicacy
and above all, that secret weapon,
the one we can't talk about.   10
Calm down, man,
the intel officer and the CO
and the border police chief
who's also a colonel in that hush-hush commando unit
are all primed for the order: Go!   15
and everything's shined up like the skin of a snake
and we've got chocolate wafers on every base
and grape juice and Tempo soda
and that's why we won't give in to terror
we will not fold in the face of violence   20
we'll never fold, no matter what
'cause our billy clubs are nice and hard.
God, who has chosen us from all the nations,
comforteth with apples
the fighting arm of the IDF,   25
and the iron boxes and the crates of fresh explosives

Title, *The Fruit of the Land* (Heb. *zimrat ha-aretz*). *Zimra* means singing; in biblical
Hebrew it can also mean "produce, bounty" (Gen. 43:11) and "power, might" (Psalm
118:14).

Line 24, *comforteth with apples*. Cf. Song of Songs 2:5, "Stay me with flagons, comfort
me with apples."

Line 25, *IDF* (Heb. *tzahal*). An acronym for *tzva ha-hagana le-yisrael*, Israel Defense
Forces.

and we've got cluster bombs too,
though of course that's off the record.
Serve us bourekas and cake, O woman of the house,
for we were slaves in the land of Egypt   30
but never again,
and blot out the remembrance of Amalek
if you can track him down,
and if you seek him without success,
Blessed be the tiny match   35
that a soldier in some crack unit will suddenly strike
and set off the whole bloody mess.

Line 29, *bourekas*. Common Middle Eastern snack made from puff pastry with a savory filling.

Line 32, *Amalek*. The biblical archenemy of Israel. Cf. Deut. 25:19, "thou shalt blot out the remembrance of Amalek from under heaven." See "Lullaby."

Line 35, *Blessed be the . . . match*. Alludes ironically to a poem written by the partisan Chana Senesh in 1944, well known today as a Hebrew song, praising the match that ignites the hearts of others even as it is consumed.

Index of Titles and First Lines